GOLF
Fundamentals

Sports Fundamentals Series

GOLF
Fundamentals

Denise St. Pierre

Human Kinetics

Library of Congress Cataloging-in-Publication Data

Golf fundamentals / Human Kinetics with Denise St. Pierre.
    p. cm. -- (Sports fundamentals series)
  ISBN 0-7360-5431-6 (soft cover)
  1. Golf. I. St. Pierre, Denise. II. Human Kinetics (Organization) III. Series.
  GV965.G5424 2004
  796.352'3--dc22

                                        2004001617

ISBN: 0-7360-5431-6

Developmental Editors: Susanna Blalock, Cynthia McEntire
Assistant Editors: Cory Weber, Kim Thoren
Copyeditor: Patsy Fortney
Proofreader: Coree Clark
Graphic Designer: Robert Reuther
Graphic Artist: Tara Welsch
Photo Manager: Dan Wendt
Cover Designer: Keith Blomberg
Photographer (cover): Dan Wendt
Photographer (interior): Kelly Huff
Art Manager: Kareema McLendon
Illustrator: Mic Greenberg
Printer: United Graphics

Human Kinetics books are available at special discounts for bulk purchase. Special editions or book excerpts can also be created to specification. For details, contact the Special Sales Manager at Human Kinetics.

Printed in the United States of America   10 9 8 7 6 5 4 3 2 1

Human Kinetics
Web site: www.HumanKinetics.com

United States: Human Kinetics
P.O. Box 5076
Champaign, IL 61825-5076
800-747-4457
e-mail: humank@hkusa.com

Canada: Human Kinetics
475 Devonshire Road Unit 100
Windsor, ON N8Y 2L5
800-465-7301 (in Canada only)
e-mail: orders@hkcanada.com

Europe: Human Kinetics
107 Bradford Road
Stanningley
Leeds LS28 6AT, United Kingdom
+44 (0) 113 255 5665
e-mail: hk@hkeurope.com

Australia: Human Kinetics
57A Price Avenue
Lower Mitcham, South Australia 5062
08 8277 1555
e-mail: liaw@hkaustralia.com

New Zealand: Human Kinetics
Division of Sports Distributors NZ Ltd.
P.O. Box 300 226 Albany
North Shore City
Auckland
0064 9 448 1207
e-mail: blairc@hknewz.com

Welcome to Sports Fundamentals

The Sports Fundamentals Series uses a learn-by-doing approach to teach those who want to play, not just read. Clear, concise instructions and illustrations make it easy to become more proficient in the game or activity, allowing readers to participate quickly and have more fun.

Between the covers, this book contains rock-solid information, precise instructions, and clear photos and illustrations that immerse readers in the sport. Each fundamental chapter is divided into four major sections:

- You Can Do It!: Jump right into the game or activity with a clear explanation of how to perform an essential skill or tactic.
- More to Choose and Use: Find out more about the skill or learn exciting alternatives.
- Take It to the Course: Apply the new skill in a game situation.
- Give It a Go: Use drills and gamelike activities to develop skills by doing and gauge learning and performance with self-tests.

No more sitting on the sidelines! The Sports Fundamentals Series gets you right into the game. Apply the techniques and tactics as they are learned, and have fun—win or lose!

Contents

Chapter 1   **The Game of Golf** 1

Chapter 2   **Equipment** 13

Chapter 3   **Putting** 25

Chapter 4   **Chipping** 39

Chapter 5   **Pitch Shots** 53

Chapter 6   **Bunker Shots** 63

Chapter 7   **Full Swing Fundamentals** 73

Chapter 8   **Full Swing With Irons** 83

Chapter 9   **Full Swing With Woods** 93

Chapter 10   **Recovery Shots** 101

Chapter 11   **Course Management** 109

Chapter 12   **Scoring and Tournaments** 123

Chapter 13   **On-Course Games** 129

About the Writer 133

The Game of Golf

Golf is a game played outdoors on some of the most spectacular landscapes all over the world. People of both genders and of all ages and abilities enjoy the game. Golf can be addictive, but it is always refreshing for those of us with the right attitude.

Throughout my years of giving lessons to beginners, I have often been amused by the reasons so many take up the game. The number one reason is curiosity. Many people want to know why their friends and family who play are so fascinated with the game. They want to know what it is about golf that brings such enjoyment and frustration at the same time.

Golf is not just a sport or a recreational game; for some of us it is a way of life. Golf is our social connection, our education when traveling to different geographical regions; for some it is even spiritual. The enticement often comes from the difficulty of the game itself. A few years ago a popular sport magazine did a survey to find out which sports are the most difficult to become proficient in. The study rated all of the skills required for participation in various sports. Golf was found to be the second most difficult sport to become proficient in; polo was number one.

Why try to learn one of the most difficult sports? Golf is the game of a lifetime. The high when you are playing well is worth laboring through the low points. The first step is deciding what you want from the game. It is my belief that everyone can learn this game with the right instruction, attention to habit formation, and willingness to stay patient during the learning process. Grantland Rice once said, "Golf is twenty percent mechanics and technique. The other eighty percent is philosophy, humor, tragedy, romance, melodrama, companionship, camaraderie, cussedness, and conversation."

Deciding to take up the game of golf or improve the golf skills you already have is the start of a great adventure. The road to mastery will be strewn with moments of connection and moments of desperation. If you can embrace the times of desperation and love the process despite the difficulty, you are on your way to a very satisfying relationship with the sport.

The golf world is filled with instructional resources to help you learn and improve your game. Many of your well-intending golf friends may give advice that is inappropriate for you. You need to decide what is best for you. A professional instructor that you can communicate with and trust is your best avenue. Ultimately, you are responsible for going after what you want. If learning golf is what you want, proceed at your own pace, take up one skill at a time, and practice for the love of it!

Golf is a unique sport in that each course presents different challenges. No two golf courses are alike. The experience of playing the game is created less by your fellow players and more by how the course challenges your skills. This may be one reason for golf's popularity. Players can vary in age from 3 to 103. Size, strength, and body type do not matter. The game provides something for everyone. According to Arnold Daly, "Golf is like a love affair. If you don't take it seriously, it's no fun. If you do take it seriously, it breaks your heart."

The History of Golf

The game of golf as we now know it started in Scotland. Shepherds who spent much of their time in the fields watching over their herds would pass the day by hitting small rocks along the terrain with sticks. Eventually a leather ball stuffed with feathers was hit into cans positioned at various spots on the ground. The first sand traps were places where animals burrowed into banks for protection from the strong winds. In time, their burrowing would wear away the grass, leaving sandy areas similar to the bunkers, or sand traps, found on today's golf courses. King James II of Scotland banned golf in 1457 because people were spending too much time playing the game and not enough time working on their archery skills.

Golf did not move to other areas of the world until the late 1700s when the first organized club was founded in southeast London. Golf courses did not come to the United States until the late 1800s. Established in 1884, The Oakhurst Links Golf Club in White Sulphur Springs, West Virginia was the first organized club in the U.S., but it is no longer in existence.

This popular leisure activity eventually turned into the game it is today, a game played by many people in various circles and venues. The game eventually developed into a structure consisting of 18 separate holes, each of which in-

1.1 A hole of golf is made up of the teeing ground, the fairway, the rough, and the green.

cludes the teeing ground, the fairway, the rough, and the green (figure 1.1). Golf is played for both leisure and competition. Some people choose golf for their occupation and compete on a professional golf tour. Today millions of people participate in the game of golf on thousands of golf courses in all parts of the world!

Golf Course

Most golf courses are made up of 18 golf holes. Play begins on hole 1 and continues through hole 18. Legend has it that the Scots came up with 18 holes because there are 18 shots in a pint of whiskey, one for each hole! The truth is, no one really knows why a course consists of 18 holes. Most courses are built so that the first 9 holes come back to the course's starting point for the benefit of the many golfers who prefer to play only 9 holes. Nine holes is typically the maximum number of holes for a new golfer to play or the desired number of holes if time is a factor.

The time needed to play an 18-hole round is usually four hours; thus two hours are needed for 9 holes. Many scorecards today list holes 1 through 9 followed by the word *out*, which means your total score for the first 9 holes played. The second half of the scorecard lists holes 10 through 18 and the word *in* for your total on the second 9 holes (figure 1.2). Today we refer to this distinction as the "front 9" and the "back 9." Golfers can usually stop to pick up a snack or drink at the completion of 9 holes if playing a full 18. Playing from the 9th hole to the 10th hole is referred to as *making the turn*. It is important to keep moving if you are playing a full round so as not to slow down the players who may be behind you. If you play 18 holes, the 18th hole will usually conclude near the clubhouse or golf shop. You can stop your round at any time when playing for recreation. Keep in mind the direction in which you are moving in case you need to find your way back to the clubhouse!

Golf holes vary in length. Usually a golf course will have shorter holes of 90 to 200 yards, medium holes of 201 to 400 yards, and longer holes of 401 to 590 yards. Yardages are measured from a marker on the tee box to the center of the green.

A score of *par* is assigned to each hole (figure 1.3, a-c). Par is considered the perfect score for the hole. Par is established based on the number of strokes needed to reach the green (given the length of the hole) with two strokes remaining to get the ball in the hole once on the putting green. Therefore, a par 4 means that it takes two shots to reach the green and two putts to put the ball in the hole. A par 3 means that you must drive the green in one stroke and then sink the ball in two putts. Keep in mind that par is a perfect score meant for those with experience and advanced skill. Professional golfers will go for par or less on every hole. Good amateur players may strive to achieve par, and recreational golfers are doing well when they achieve two or fewer strokes over par.

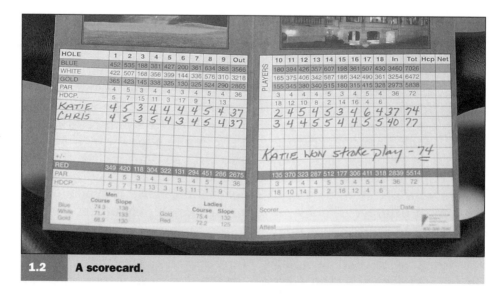

1.2   A scorecard.

4

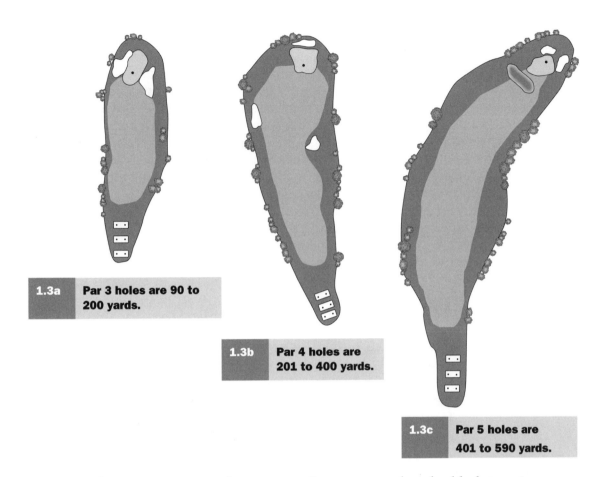

1.3a Par 3 holes are 90 to 200 yards.

1.3b Par 4 holes are 201 to 400 yards.

1.3c Par 5 holes are 401 to 590 yards.

A *bogey* is a score of one more than par, and a *double bogey* is two more than par. For example, a score of five strokes on a par 4 hole would be a bogey. A double bogey is a score of six strokes on a par 4 hole. A score of one stroke less than par is called a *birdie*. For example, if a golfer made a score of 3 on a par 4 hole, it would be a birdie. A score of two strokes less than par is called an *eagle*. A score of 2 on a par 4 hole would be an eagle.

In many sports, such as basketball and football, the challenge comes from the opponent. In contrast, the main opponent in golf is the course itself. The challenge is to compete against par and the design of the course. Some golf courses have only par 3 holes. A par 3 course is not as enticing to more serious players, but generally is very good for new golfers, young children, or older players because of the shorter length of the total course. A regulation course usually includes four par 3 holes, four par 5 holes, and ten par 4 holes. A typical total par for 18 holes, then, is 72. Total par can vary from 70 to 75, depending on the course. A player does not have to play the full 18 holes. Some players prefer 9 holes because of their skill level or time constraints. In fact, some courses offer only 9 holes.

Teeing Ground

Each hole begins at the tee area, which is referred to as the *teeing ground* or *tee box*. The teeing ground is a raised rectangular area of closely mown grass from which the golfer hits the first shot for that hole. On the tee area is a set of markers referred to as *tee markers*. The tee markers designate where the ball is to be played from on the tee. You must tee your ball up between the markers and no more than two club lengths back from them. If you tee your ball up in front of the markers, you are penalized one stroke.

Each teeing ground contains three to four sets of tee markers. Each set designates a certain yardage to the green from that particular point (figure 1.4). A forward tee box would be the closest tee marker or the shortest distance to play the hole. A back tee box would indicate the farthest distance the hole can be played. In between the forward tee box and the back tee box is the middle tee box. The forward tee boxes are sometimes called the *ladies' tees;* the middle tee boxes, the *men's tees;* and the back tee boxes, the *championship tees* or *professional tees.* In recent years teaching professionals have been encouraging players to describe the different areas as *forward, middle,* and *back.* Most women will tee off from the forward teeing areas because they are generally less powerful distance hitters than most men. However, the women on the professional and collegiate levels will play from mostly middle tee boxes based on their ability

1.4   The yardage sign found on the teeing ground of each hole gives the distances from the various sets of tee markers to the pin.

to hit the ball farther, thus keeping the game challenging. Most men will tee from the middle to back tee boxes. Young golfers just taking up the game are encouraged to begin at the forward tee box areas.

Players should decide where to begin the hole based on the distance they are capable of hitting the ball. The teeing ground is the only place on the course where a player is allowed to put the ball on a tee, which is usually a wooden peg one and a half inches long (figure 1.5).

As you stand on the teeing ground, be sure to look at the design of the golf hole. The fairway may lie straight ahead, or it may turn to the right or left at almost a 90-degree angle, which is referred to as a *dogleg* (figure 1.6). Some holes, particularly par 5s, may have fairways that dogleg right then dogleg left before the green. The positioning of bunkers, trees, and hazards will help you decide where to hit the ball.

1.5 The teeing ground is the only place on the course where a golfer is allowed to put the ball on a tee.

Fairway and Rough

Each hole consists of a fairway defined by a closely mown area of grass that leads to the putting green. The fairway is the ideal area from which to hit your golf ball. Sticks, leaves, or anything not fixed or growing are considered *loose impediments* and may be moved away from your ball when it is lying in the fairway or rough areas. You may *not* remove loose impediments when hitting from a hazard (a sand bunker or water hazard). The rough lines the fairway and is defined by a longer cut of grass; it is typically not as desirable an area from which to hit your ball. When hitting from either the fairway or the rough, you may create a *divot* by removing a piece of grass during your swing. This grass should be replaced when possible. Some courses provide a sand and seed mixture for you to use when replacing your divots.

1.6 Hole with a dogleg to the right.

The rough or fairway may sometimes consist of sand bunkers, which help define the shape of the fairways and rough areas. Sand bunkers are considered hazards. You are not allowed to ground your club in a hazard. *Grounding* is when you touch your club to the surface of the hazard prior to hitting your shot. You should hold the club just above the sand or surface of the hazard prior to your shot. If you breach this rule, you will have an additional two strokes added to your score for the hole. Hazards may also be streams, ponds, or lakes that will line or cut across a fairway, adding to the difficulty of the hole. Adding to the beauty of fairways and rough areas can also be trees, rocks, or any other natural features. (Desert courses, lined with cacti, are quite different from courses in the Northeast, which typically have fairways lined with large trees.)

Green

The green is the "hallowed" ground. It is the closest mown area of the golf course specifically designed to roll a ball into a small opening or *cup.* The putting green is very delicate and must be treated with respect. Never take a full golf swing on the putting green. Shots taken on a putting green are meant to roll the ball, not send it into the air. When walking across a green, walk gently so as not to scuff or mark the green in any way.

The area can take on many shapes, but it is usually rounded. Sand bunkers can surround greens, further defining their shape. These bunkers are known as greenside bunkers.

The hole that is cut into the green is four and a half inches in diameter and at least four inches deep. A flag is inserted into the hole to indicate the location from a distance. When players are putting into the hole, the flagstick is removed and placed away from the playing area. If the flagstick is touched by a ball that is on the green while putting, the player incurs a two-stroke penalty. A flag can be left in the hole when it is necessary to see the hole, but should be tended by another player so it can be removed after the ball has been hit.

The player farthest from the hole should putt first. All other players should pick up their balls and mark the spot with a ball marker or flat object such as a coin. If a player strikes another player's ball while putting on the green, the player incurs a two-stroke penalty. To help with the pace of play, a player whose ball lies close to the hole may ask to *putt out* (finish the hole) rather than mark the ball. Be sure not to stand between any player and the hole. When the last player has putted, the flag should be promptly returned to the hole by the first player to finish the hole. Always place your clubs on the side of the green, toward the next hole to be played.

Rules and Etiquette

The object of the game is to hit the ball from the tee box to the fairway and then to the green. Players proceed down the fairway, with the player whose ball is farthest from the hole playing first. Players should have an idea of the general direction of their ball and move toward that direction ready to hit when it is their turn. It is important to keep play moving. If a group behind you is waiting to play, always let them play through, provided you are not waiting on a group in front of you. This is common golf etiquette.

Some players prefer to take a practice swing prior to hitting the shot. This is permissible, but only one practice swing is necessary when making a full swing. Any attempt to hit the ball counts as a stroke whether the ball moves forward or not. A *whiff*, which is a swing that misses the ball, is still counted as one stroke.

If the ball becomes lost during the course of play, the player incurs a penalty of one stroke and puts another ball in play from where the original ball was first played. Thus, the penalty for a lost ball is referred to as *stroke and distance.* The same rule applies for a ball hit out of bounds. The boundaries on a golf course are marked by white stakes. If a ball goes beyond the white stakes, it is out of bounds and cannot be played. A stroke and distance penalty is incurred.

Water hazards can also come into play during the course of a hole. A water hazard is marked with red or yellow stakes. A yellow-staked hazard is a direct water hazard. A red-staked hazard is a lateral water hazard. If your ball goes into the water hazard, you can play out of the hazard if it is feasible. Usually you will have to drop another ball near the hazard and count a penalty stroke for doing so. There are four options for dropping your ball from a lateral hazard and two options for dropping your ball from a direct hazard. (Refer to the *USGA Rules of Golf* handbook for the proper procedures for dropping a ball from a hazard.) In contrast, if your ball ends up on or near a man-made obstruction (cart paths, sprinkler heads, benches), you may move the ball without penalty. You must first take your stance and swing at the nearest point of relief that is not closer to the hole but away from the obstruction, measure one club length from the position, and drop your ball. You may proceed to play your shot without having to take a penalty stroke. If the obstruction is movable, simply remove the obstruction and proceed to play your shot.

Play continues down the hole until all players are on the green. Once all players are on the green, the player farthest from the hole putts first. The hole is complete when the ball falls into the cup. A total number of strokes is recorded for each hole played. The challenge is to get the ball in the hole with the least number of strokes. If you are keeping score, write down your score at the next tee box while your competitors hit their tee shots. This will also help with the pace of play.

Playing on the course for the first time can be intimidating. Remember that you do not have to keep score or hit the ball each time. Just being out on the course and learning the art of playing the game are enough to get you started.

If you are new to the sport of golf, your skills may not allow you to keep up with the field. You may be tempted at this point to give up the game. You may be afraid that you are not capable of playing because you need more time to reach the green and put the ball in the hole. It is poor etiquette to keep a group behind you waiting for a long time. Here is an idea to speed up play your first few times on the course. If the hole you are about to play is a par 4, give yourself four shots to get within 50 yards of the green. If you are not within 50 yards of the green after four shots, pick up the ball and place it within 50 yards of the green. Give yourself four more shots to put the ball into the hole. If you have not reached the hole in the next four shots, proceed to the next hole. This keeps your group moving, and you get course experience without feeling pressure from your group or the group behind you to finish the hole. This is strictly a practice method to help you get used to playing the game; do not use this method in a league or tournament setting. Some league play may require you to take a maximum score of 10 on any given hole to help keep play moving. In other words, you must hit every shot and not pick up the ball unless you have already hit the ball 10 times. A new player who can score double par or better on any given hole is well on the way to playing with proficiency.

Most golf courses require you to call ahead to schedule a time to play. You will be given a tee time based on availability. Tee times for groups are spaced from 7 minutes to 10 minutes apart. The maximum number of players in a group is four (a foursome). If you are playing with only one other person, you would be considered a twosome. When golf courses are busy, they often put two twosomes together at the same tee time.

Step Onto the Course

Now that you have a general idea about the game, how can you learn the skills you need to play? Each of us is unique. We process information differently according to our own styles. The child's way of thinking is experiencing, doing, responding, and mimicking. A child's play is all learning. As we learn to intellectualize and become more analytical, we tend to get stuck when processing information.

In golf we must first learn the mechanics of the swing by making proper habits of the fundamentals. Habits are those things we do without conscious direction from our brains. We need to make "swing habits" so that we can play the game without thinking about our technique. We learn to store information by memory, which is made up of things we have seen, felt, heard, smelled, and tasted. Muscle memory is not possible. It is our brain that remembers and is able to turn the sensory images into recognizable perceptions.

What is it that allows us to type or write a letter, drive a car, or ride a bicycle without falling? The actual transfer from conscious thought to the automatic or subconscious state of doing without thinking is remarkably easy. Exercise scientists have found, through research studies of people learning motor skills, that habits are formed when people focus their attention and intention on the task at hand 60 times a day for 21 days in a row. The key element is the 21 days in a row. Practicing only when you have a lot of time is not conducive to making solid habits. A small amount of practice over a period of consecutive days is much more likely to result in success.

Ideally you want your skills to become habits so you can concentrate on managing your game while playing the golf course. One of the best ways to create good swing habits is through drill practice. You will find several drills in the different chapters of this book to help build your golf swing and move you on your way to playing the game with enjoyment. To make the reading suitable for both right- and left-handed players, I use the words *target* and *trail* instead of *right* and *left*. For a right-handed player the target side is the left side or the side closest to the target when setting up to hit a shot. The trail side is the side farthest from the target when setting up to hit a shot, which for the right-handed player would be the right side.

Remember that learning is a lifelong process. In his book *Mastery*, George Leonard writes that improvement in learning does not follow a progressive line upward. The line has plateaus and sometimes down curves along the way. This cannot be more true than in learning the game of golf. Leonard mentions that the key is loving the process even on the plateaus. This is usually when most people give up out of frustration or boredom. Moving through this process is when you are truly on your way to learning and improvement. Remember, you have your lifetime to play the game. Enjoy!

Equipment

Specific equipment is required for most activities. Golf is no exception. An experienced golfer will notice signs that another player is new to the game. We comically call these "signs of a hacker." *Hacker* is a term used to identify a player with very little skill or lack of knowledge about the game. Signs of a hacker may include a disorganized golf bag, no headcovers on the woods, a ball retriever in the bag, a towel that clips onto the bag, a string of beads to count strokes, clothing more appropriate for jogging than for golf, a golf glove on each hand, and sandals or street shoes. Hackers also often carry the bag by the small handle rather than using the larger strap over the shoulder. If you want to look the part in the golf world, consider these signs of more experienced players: a bag with the clubs organized in the appropriate compartments, a towel loosely draped over the bag, headcovers on the woods, a colored short-sleeved shirt usually made of soft cotton, tailored shorts or pants, golf shoes, and one glove on the target hand. Experienced players also carry the bag using the larger strap over the shoulder.

Golf equipment can be expensive. Today the consumer has many more options in regard to clubs, shoes, and balls. At one time pro shops at golf facilities were the only places to purchase equipment. Now golfers can shop at golf houses, large discount stores that carry equipment at lower prices. The trade-off can be the personal attention and expert advice you receive from purchasing through the local golf professional at the golf course. Members of private golf clubs customarily support the golf professionals at the club.

To get started in the game, you will need a set of clubs, golf balls, tees, and a towel. Anything beyond that is simply accessorizing and not necessary. As an instructor of the game, I have seen many new students arrive at their first lesson with a borrowed set of clubs or an old passed-on set not suited for them. The rubber grip end of every club is where you need to hold on. This will usually wear down over a one- to two-year period. Most used sets of clubs are 10 or more years old and have never had the grips replaced. At the very least, if you are using an old set of clubs, invest in a new set of grips. Most golf shops replace grips for as little as $6 a club. Having the proper equipment can greatly help the novice player succeed in the beginning stages of learning the game. By looking the part and having the proper equipment, you will be well on your way to success.

Clubs

Before the 1930s wealthy golfers would put as many as 30 clubs in their bags. Because every club has a specific design and purpose, the advantage often went to the person with more tools to work with. As a result, the United States Golf Association (USGA) created a limit of 14 clubs in a bag to make the game more competitive for poorer golfers (figure 2.1). A beginning golfer does not need a full set of 14

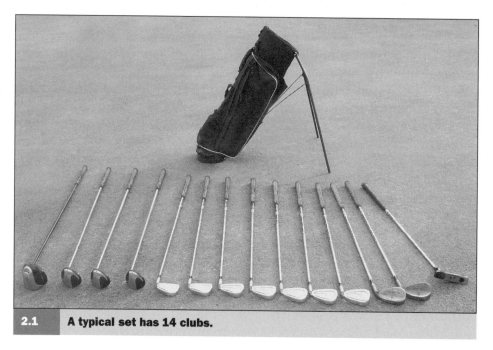

2.1   **A typical set has 14 clubs.**

clubs to play the game at first. A typical set includes three or four woods, seven irons numbered 3 through 9, a pitching wedge, a sand wedge, and a putter. Today more golfers are adding a third wedge, called a lob wedge, to their bags.

Clubs are composed of three main parts: the grip, the shaft, and the clubface (figure 2.2). Clubs vary in length, lie angle, and loft angle. The length of a club ranges from approximately 44 inches to 30 inches depending on the individual set and the individual user. The woods are the longest clubs in the set, and the putter is the shortest. The *lie angle* of the club is the distance from the shaft centerline and the sole of the golf club as it is placed on the ground. The lie angle of a set of clubs should be matched. In other words, all clubs in a set should have the same lie angle. Lie angle is determined by your size, type of swing, and body type. The *loft angle*, on the other hand, changes from club to club. Each club has a specific loft angle to help launch the ball a certain height in the air, thus affecting the

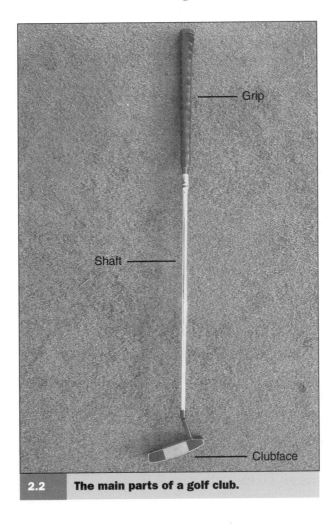

Grip

Shaft

Clubface

2.2   **The main parts of a golf club.**

distance the ball will travel. The loft angle is the distance between the clubface and the shaft.

Because woods are the longest clubs in a set, they typically allow for the most distance (1, 3, 5, 7, or 9). The 1 wood is referred to as the *driver* because it is used only to start a hole from the teeing ground. The other woods (3, 4, 5, 7, and 9) are called *fairway woods*. They are used when a player needs more distance to carry the ball while on the fairway. Fairway woods are sometimes used from the teeing ground on shorter holes such as par 3s because the driver would send the ball too far. Years ago woods actually were made of wood, but today they are made of steel, titanium, or aluminum. Nevertheless, we still refer to them as wood-type clubs.

A typical set of irons contains the 3, 4, 5, 6, 7, 8, and 9 irons as well as the pitching, sand, and lob wedges (figure 2.3). The lower the number of the club, the longer the shaft is and the less loft the clubface has (figure 2.4). A less lofted club will allow the ball to fly lower and farther. The highest lofted, and shortest, club is the lob wedge, which is used primarily around the green or from a very short distance to the green.

The main difference between a sand wedge and a pitching wedge is the size of the sole of the club. The sand wedge (figure 2.5) will have a *flange* on the bottom designed to make the clubhead heavier and easier to move through the sand, rather than a typical wedge, which may dig into the sand, resulting in the ball remaining in the sand.

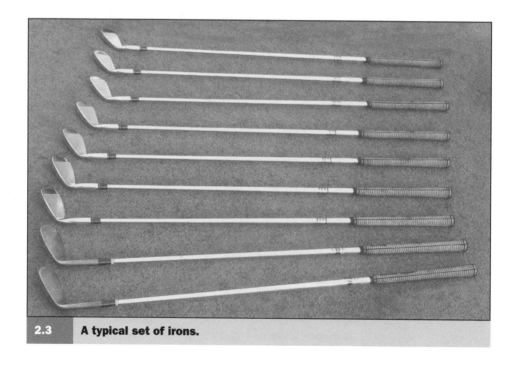

2.3 **A typical set of irons.**

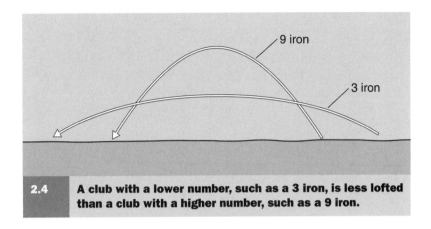

2.4 | A club with a lower number, such as a 3 iron, is less lofted than a club with a higher number, such as a 9 iron.

2.5 | The sand wedge.

The putter is quite different from the other clubs (figure 2.6). There are as many designs in putters as there are types of golfers. It is not uncommon for a golfer who has played the game for 10 years to have had 10 different putters. Putters are designed to roll the ball when it is on the green. They are generally the shortest of all the clubs and have the least amount of loft. (Most putters have between 1 and 2 degrees of loft.) Because almost half of the strokes in a round of golf are from putting, this club is very important to the golfer. Golfers typically try various putters before finding the one

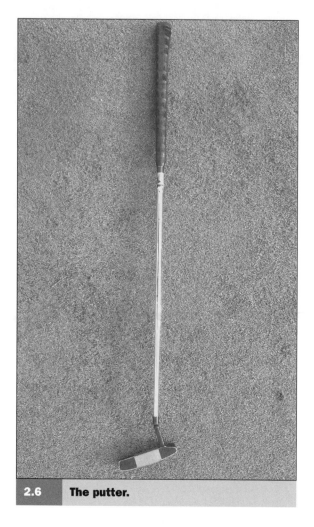

that is best suited to their style of putting. The most noticeable difference between the putter and the rest of the clubs is the grip. The grip of a putter is flat on the top of the shaft to allow the hands to sit comfortably on the grip without having to exert much pressure to hold the club (figure 2.7).

Shafts are made of different materials, allowing the overall weight of the club to change. A graphite shaft is lighter overall than a steel shaft. This can help a weaker player generate more clubhead speed, resulting in greater distance. Most woods are designed with graphite or titanium shafts for this reason. The amount of swing speed you generate will influence the flexibility of your shaft. A strong, fast swing may require a stiffer shaft, and a slower swing may require a more flexible shaft. Having clubs that match your specifications is very important. A new player may not see a great difference at first with a fitted set; however, a set made to your specifications may enable you to see improvement much faster.

Golf clubs vary in as many ways as golfers do. When you can make a fairly consistent golf swing, you may want to buy clubs that are professionally fitted. Clubs can be designed to match and enhance your swing according to your specifications.

Most tour professionals will hit the ball 50 to 100 yards farther with a given club. Most top female amateurs and professionals will also hit the ball 50 to 100 yards farther than the average woman can hit. Once you have a consistent swing, you should learn how far you hit with each club. As noted in table 2.1, there is a 10-yard difference between clubs that are one up or down from each other in number and degree.

2.7 **The grip of the putter.**

Table 2.1

CLUB DEGREES AND DISTANCES

Type of club	Loft of face	Men's average recreational distance	Women's average recreational distance
1 wood	10 degrees	250 yards	160 yards
3 wood	15 degrees	225 yards	135 yards
5 wood	20 degrees	200 yards	115 yards
3 iron	22 degrees	190 yards	105 yards
4 iron	25 degrees	180 yards	95 yards
5 iron	28 degrees	170 yards	85 yards
6 iron	32 degrees	160 yards	75 yards
7 iron	36 degrees	150 yards	65 yards
8 iron	40 degrees	140 yards	55 yards
9 iron	44 degrees	130 yards	45 yards
Pitching wedge	48 degrees	120 yards	35 yards
Sand wedge	53 degrees	110 yards	25 yards
Lob wedge	56 to 60 degrees	100 yards	15 yards

The amount of distance will vary from player to player. These represent average distances.

Balls

We have come a long way in the construction and technology of the golf ball since the days of balls made of feathers and leather. The golf ball has evolved into a Surlyn or balata covering with small indentations called *dimples* over a wound rubber or solid core depending on the type of ball. Buying golf balls can be as confusing as purchasing golf clubs. There are so many balls to choose from. To keep it simple, golf balls fall into two categories: wound and solid (two-piece). A wound ball has more spin, thus allowing the golfer to stop the ball more easily on the green. A solid ball has less spin, which slows for more distance, making it more popular among recreational players and players who have a tendency to hit the ball shorter. Most golf ball packages have the specifications written on them.

Compression is also a factor in the makeup of golf balls. Compression is the measurement of ball stiffness related to how much the ball will deflect or flatten when struck by the clubface. How much the ball compresses from the face of the club determines the spin rate of the ball. A golfer with a fast swing speed will generally play with a 90 to 100 compression ball. A golfer with a slower swing speed will be better off playing with an 80 to 90 compression ball. The compression of the ball is written on the ball itself or on the packaging.

Clothing and Shoes

Another important piece of equipment is golf shoes. Golf shoes have cleats on the sole of the shoe to keep the feet from slipping during the swing. This is especially helpful when playing in wet conditions. Golf shoes are not imperative, however. Many recreational golfers wear a sturdy athletic shoe for comfort rather than a golf shoe. Some manufacturers of golf shoes have begun designing a golf shoe that is similar to a sneaker. Years ago golfers wore metal-spiked shoes. Most golf courses today require every golfer to have soft-spiked shoes, which are all that are sold today.

Most important is that the shoes fit your feet and support you during movement. The shoes you wear on a golf course can affect your balance during your swing and your level of fatigue at the end of your round. If you are wearing shoes that do not support your feet, you may be working harder to keep your balance during play.

A standard joke among those who do not play the game is that golf is the only game in which you can get away with wearing stripes and plaids on the same day. Although it is a game that affords many outrageous styles, it is a ladies' and gentlemen's game expected to be played by those who are well-dressed for it. An appropriately dressed golfer will wear soft cotton clothing of matching top and bottoms (figure 2.8). The shirt for men should have a collar. At some golf courses the length of shorts for women can be no higher than four inches from the knee. Jeans are almost never worn on most private golf courses. Bathing suits and jogging clothes are not appropriate attire. Your clothes should be comfortable and provide maximum range of motion, while showing style and class.

The golf glove is another article of clothing that can be helpful to the player. Years ago the grips on golf clubs were made of leather. The leather would become worn and very slippery. Players wore a glove on the target hand to keep the club from slipping during the swing. Because most grips are made of rubber today, which generally provides a less slippery surface, a glove is not necessary. However, many players believe that wearing a glove gives them a better hold on the club. If you swing right-handed, wear a glove on your left hand. If you swing left-handed, wear a glove on your right hand. A

2.8 **A well-dressed golfer.**

golf glove should fit snugly but comfortably on your hand. When putting or chipping, most experienced players will remove the glove to allow for more feel on the club. Because these shots do not require a fast-moving swing motion, players can easily keep hold of the club. Golf gloves come in various sizes and can be purchased in most golf shops in the country.

Other Equipment

Some other standard equipment used in the game of golf includes a golf bag, tees, a golf towel, and a divot tool. Your clubs are carried in a golf bag (figure 2.9). The type of bag you choose may depend on whether you play the game walking or riding. Golf bags come in various sizes and weights. Generally, a carry bag will be lighter in weight, have two straps to distribute the weight evenly on your back, and include a few pockets to carry balls, tees, and a glove. If you plan to ride in a cart when you play, you can have as big a bag as you think you need. Golf professionals have caddies who carry large bags to accommodate extra clothes and towels.

2.9 A golf bag.

Organize your golf bag. Place balls and tees in separate pockets. Place your golf glove in a plastic baggie to ensure further longevity of the glove. Place your longest clubs (woods) in the tallest section of the bag. The 3, 4, and 5 irons go together in the middle. The 6, 7, and 8 irons go together in the middle. The 9 iron, pitching wedge, sand wedge, and putter go in the bottom of the bag. This allows you to get to your clubs easily. Use headcovers on your woods. When woods really were made of wood, the headcovers protected them from chipping and dampness. Now woods are made mostly from metals that hold up under these conditions. Headcovers are still used, however, to give a finished appearance to a set of clubs.

Another piece of equipment is the tee, which is usually made of wood and ranges in size from one inch to two and a half inches. The size of the tee will depend on your personal preference. When teeing up your ball while using the driver, half of your ball should be above the golf club when it is placed behind the ball on the tee and half should be below. When using a tee with an iron, the tee should be significantly lower because the swing with the irons allows for the ball to be struck at the bottom of the swing arc rather than on the upswing as with the woods.

After using a club, you should use a golf towel to wipe off its face. A clubface that has dirt or grass stuck to it is at a disadvantage if used in this condition. The small lines on your clubface cause the ball to spin. The towel is also used for cleaning off your golf ball once you are on the green. Because the green is the only place where you can mark and lift your ball, it is the perfect place to clean your golf ball. A clean golf ball will have a better roll to the hole and thus a better chance of going in the hole. This is why an experienced player will have a towel that is not clipped to the bag. A towel that is simply draped over the clubs can be brought onto the putting green where it is quite useful.

A divot tool is used to repair any marks that your ball may leave on the putting surface. This tool is the best $5 or $10 investment you can make. When a golf ball falls onto the green, it usually makes a small hole or mark. By repairing the hole with the divot tool, you ensure that the green will grow back to its original state in less than 48 hours. To use the divot tool, place it into the green and twist (figure 2.10). A good rule of thumb is to repair your ball mark and one more if you find one. A ball mark that is not repaired can take up to two weeks to heal provided it is taken care of by the green's superintendent. Many divot tools also have a ball marker attached to them, which can be helpful in marking your golf ball to distinguish your ball from those of your playing competitors.

Having the proper equipment can make all the difference in your enjoyment of the game. Be sure to seek out professional advice when

Repairing a divot with a divot tool.

purchasing golf clubs and shoes. Your choice of golf bag will depend on your needs and how you plan to play the game, walking or riding. You can purchase a golf glove, towel, balls, divot tool, and tees at most sporting goods stores. Making the investment in the right equipment is a step toward your commitment to learn and enjoy the game for your lifetime!

Putting

"Drive for show, putt for dough" is a common phrase heard in many golf circles. It is also common to watch a golf tournament and hear the announcer whisper, "If she makes this putt, she will secure the championship!" or, "If he makes this putt, he will tie the leader and force a playoff!" Putting is the smallest form of the golf swing. It is the last thing a player does to complete the hole, and ironically it is the first step in learning the golf swing. In a round of golf approximately 43 percent of the total strokes taken come from putting. When a student wants to lower her score, the first question I ask is, "How many putts do you average in a round?" Ideally you want to have two or fewer putts per hole played.

Putting is an art. Players must use sound mechanics to properly stroke the ball on a particular line and to a particular distance. They must also be able to view the surface of the green to determine if and how much the green slopes, in which direction it slopes, and how fast or slow the ball will roll on the given surface. The good news is that everyone can become proficient at putting. Putting does not require strength or flexibility, both of which are factors in hitting the golf ball long. Therefore, some call putting "the great equalizer." We can all be good putters with a little experience reading greens and practice developing a proper stroke to control the distance and direction of our putts. In this book we build your golf swing from the shortest stroke up to the longest stroke.

Putt

The putt is the simplest stroke in golf because it requires the fewest movements. To keep your body still, you must be in a solid position before making the stroke. Begin by holding the putter comfortably around the handle, palms facing each other, thumbs pointing straight down the shaft to the head of the putter (figure 3.1). The top of the putter grip is flat to accommodate the hands comfortably with the thumbs positioned down toward the green.

The flat spot on the bottom of the clubhead should rest flat against the surface of the green (figure 3.2). Like all golf clubs, the putter has a *sweet spot,* the weighted area of the club that allows the golf ball to spring off the face of the club. The sweet spot usually is indicated by a dot or line on the top of the putter's head. A putter is set against the green with the sweet spot directly behind the center of the ball.

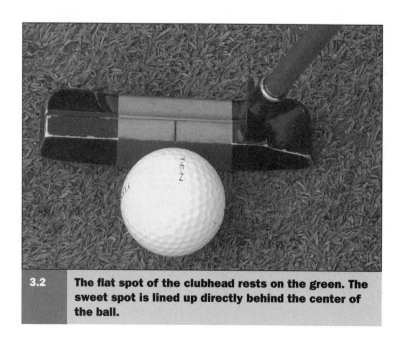

3.2   The flat spot of the clubhead rests on the green. The sweet spot is lined up directly behind the center of the ball.

In the stance (figure 3.3a), your eyes should be directly over the golf ball. Bend from the waist as far as you are comfortable and so that your arms can hang freely. Legs and arms are slightly bent and free of tension. Feet are shoulder-width apart or slightly wider for proper balance. Stroke the ball with your shoulders and arms moving together in a pendulum motion (figure 3.3b). The key is to move only your shoulders and arms, keeping the rest of your body still. Your hands and arms move together to create the pendulum. For most putts, you will stay close to the surface of the green. Longer putts require more of a swing, which brings the putter away from the surface of the green in an arc—just like the golf swing.

Many recreational golfers commit the common mistake of moving their hands more than their arms, creating an inconsistent stroke and strike of the golf ball. Remember, the key to putting is to keep your legs, hands, head, and torso still while moving your shoulders and arms in a rocking motion to create a pendulum with the putter.

3.3a   Address the ball.

3.3b   Swing with a pendulum motion.

Many elements of the putting stance and stroke will vary among golfers. For example, postures will vary depending on the size and comfort of the golfer, and the degree of bend at the waist will vary depending on the height and arm length of the golfer. The basics of the stroke, however, remain the same. Stay relaxed, keep your eyes over the ball, and keep your body still throughout the motion.

Grip Variations   Variations in putting grip styles are the overlap grip, reverse overlap grip, 10-finger grip, and the more popular cross-handed grip. The type of grip you use will depend on your preference. In all of the grip variations, the thumbs are positioned down the shaft pointing toward the green. In an overlap grip, the pinky of the trail hand overlaps the index finger of the target hand (figure 3.4a). In the reverse overlap grip, the index finger of the target hand overlaps the pinky of the trail hand (figure 3.4b). The 10-finger grip is simply both hands placed with all fingers on the grip similar to holding a baseball bat (figure 3.4c). For the cross-handed grip, place your hands at opposite positions on the club. In other words, your trail hand is high on the grip and your target hand is low on the grip. This helps stabilize the target wrist and promotes a one-lever or pendulum motion. The most important aspect of the grip is that you keep the pressure constant and light, and that your hands work together as one unit.

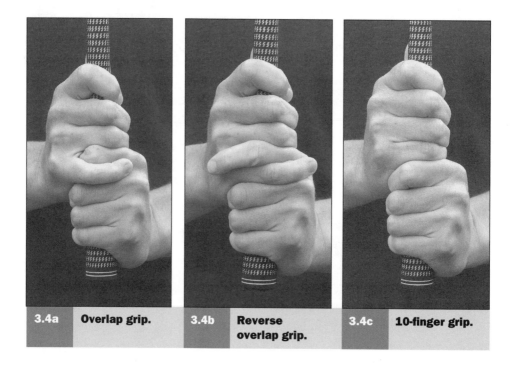

| 3.4a | Overlap grip. | 3.4b | Reverse overlap grip. | 3.4c | 10-finger grip. |

Length and Direction   In every putt the player must determine two factors: the distance the ball must travel to the hole and the direction of the putt. Distance is more important than direction. A ball that rolls the correct distance to the hole but not in the correct line usually will still be relatively close to the hole. Yet a ball traveling on the right line but not the right distance can be too short or too far, leaving the next putt far from the hole.

Distance is controlled by the length of the stroke and the contact off the face of the putter. If you were tossing the ball to the hole, how much arm swing would you need to reach the desired distance? When you're putting the ball, your putting stroke should be the same length as your arm swing if you were tossing the ball to the hole. The back swing and forward swing are similar in length, just as they would be if you were tossing the ball underhand and rolling it into the hole. For example, if the putter comes back six inches, the putter should then move forward through the ball six inches. This rule will help you produce an even-paced stroke.

The count or beat of a swing remains consistent with all strokes of all lengths. A short putt does not mean you should slow down the motion, nor does a longer putt mean you should speed up the motion. Keep your pace consistent with the different distances. The extended length of the stroke will provide greater speed through the ball and allow the ball to roll the greater distance. The ball also must consistently be struck on the sweet spot of the clubface, which will give the ball the most energy. If the ball comes off the toe of the club, the putt will tend to roll shorter. Keeping your hands and body still and moving only your arms and shoulders will ensure more consistent contact with the sweet spot of the clubface.

The direction the ball rolls is directly influenced by the face angle of the putter. The ball will travel in whatever direction the face is pointed. To keep the putt moving in the desired direction, the clubface must be aligned perpendicular to the target line and remain in that position when it strikes the golf ball. The putter will move in a small arc but always with the face moving in the direction of the target when it strikes the ball. A solid putting stroke that allows very little movement with the exception of the arms and shoulders will help keep the putter face in line.

Reading the Green

Often the putting surface will have slopes and hills of various angles. These can sometimes be the result of the design of the golf course or simply the natural elements of the topography of the land the course is built on. The act of looking at your line to the hole is called *reading the green.* When you read the green, you are looking for any unusual slopes between your ball and the hole. Walk to the hole when you first approach the green and look back at your ball. Look around the golf hole and note if the ground slopes left or right or up or down toward the hole. Keep in mind that a ball that moves slowly will be influenced by gravity and therefore curve more down the hill. A ball that is moving fast will not have a chance for gravity to pull it down the hill. The direction of the putt is in relationship to the slope of the green. Determine the high spot on the green by walking the line of your putt up to the hole. Slopes on greens typically follow the terrain of the hole as well. Be sure to look at the entire green as you approach it. Very often you can get a picture of the entire slope of the surface. Because gravity will pull the ball down the hill, aim high on the slope to allow for gravity to pull the ball down the slope once the ball begins to slow down toward the hole.

A line is defined by two points. In putting, point A is the golf ball, and point B is the spot you need to send your ball toward given the slope. The idea is to make every putt a straight line regardless of whether it is a straight line to the hole or a straight line five inches to the right of the hole. The putter face should rest perpendicular to the target line, with the sweet spot of the putter directly behind the center of the ball. As long as the clubface remains square or perpendicular to the target line through the ball, the ball should roll toward the intended target. Keep in mind that any movement of your hands or body can change the alignment of the putter face and misdirect the ball.

To recap, when putting, you must determine what line the ball will travel on, where your intended target is, and how much swing you need to use to move the ball to the hole. The green shown in figure 3.5 slopes left to right and the ball needs to travel 30 feet. To make up for gravity pulling the ball down the hill as it begins to slow down close to the hole, you should aim to the left on a straight line and allow gravity to take the ball down the hill and into the hole.

The variation of the green is truly what makes putting interesting and challenging. Every putt does not follow a straight line into the hole, yet every putt should be lined up to a point that creates a

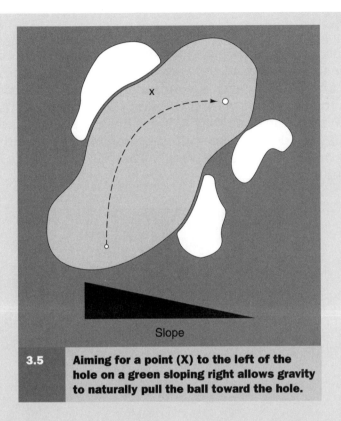

Slope

| 3.5 | Aiming for a point (X) to the left of the hole on a green sloping right allows gravity to naturally pull the ball toward the hole. |

straight line. The point may not line up directly to the hole because the slope of the green will cause the ball to curve toward the target. Learning to adjust to the slopes and speed of the green is a sure way to become a great putter.

Give it a go

When practicing putting, separate the stroke from the target. Practice the following drills to perfect your putting motion before trying to put the ball in the hole. As mentioned earlier, making a habit of any skill requires repetition. Be sure to give your full attention to one thing at a time. Using a golf hole when you are still learning the stroke can get frustrating. You begin to evaluate the wrong things. By sticking to one aspect at a time (in this case, the stroke), you will learn more quickly. Once your stroke has become a habit, you will no longer have to think about it all the time. You can play the game with all of your attention on the target instead.

THE STROKE

This is a great drill to help you make more of a pendulum motion. Place your target hand all the way to the end of the grip. Hold the grip up against the forearm of your target arm. Hold the putter and your arm together with your trail hand. Make the putting motion, using your arms and shoulders to move the putter back and through (figure 3.6). The idea is to keep the grip end of the putter up against your forearm throughout the stroke. This will help create the habit of a pendulum motion.

3.6 **Stroke drill.**

BALL TO BALL

For this drill you will need three golf balls. Place two of the balls any distance apart. (It's wise to start out about three feet apart.) Place the third ball exactly between the two but out to the side so that you can stroke the ball without hitting either of the other two

3.7	Ball-to-ball drill.

balls (figure 3.7). Take the putter back as far as the first ball and then follow through to the second ball. This drill will help promote an even-paced putting motion by keeping the back swing and the forward swing equal.

LADDER

The next three drills are distance-control drills. Having accurate distance control when putting will eliminate having more than two putts per hole. Practicing distance-control drills with various targets will help create the feel for the amount of swing needed to roll the ball the desired distance.

For the ladder drill (figure 3.8), place three tees in the green 10 feet apart. Stand five feet away from the first tee, put a ball on the ground, and stroke the ball to the tee. Aiming is not important; you want to focus only on the distance to the target. Consider it a successful putt if you stroke the ball to the tee or just slightly past it. Continue the drill by stroking the next ball to the middle target and finally to the last target. Repeat the drill and work toward 10 successful reps to the three distances. You will soon begin to feel the length of the stroke needed for longer and shorter putts. This drill can also be modified to do at home on a carpet using coins rather than tees to identify your distances.

3.8 **Ladder drill.**

SEMICIRCLE

Place six tees in a semicircle around a hole. Each tee should be approximately one foot from the hole. When you are putting toward the hole, the tees will be behind the hole and just to the left and right sides (figure 3.9). The object is to putt the ball so it either rolls into the cup or just inside the semicircle. Making the target bigger will take pressure off your putts and allow more balls to end up close to the hole. Remember, you want to put the ball in the hole in two putts or fewer while playing the game.

3.9 **Semicircle drill.**

FRINGE

The fringe is the area around the green where the grass is just a bit higher; it outlines the shape of the putting surface. Stand on a green and putt balls from the same starting point to the fringe. Move around in a complete circle, putting in all directions to the fringe. The object is to stop the golf ball just before it hits the fringe. Because greens are irregular in shape, you should find several different distances to putt the ball from the same spot. This drill is used for creating a feel for different distances.

AROUND THE WORLD

For the around-the-world drill, place five or six balls three feet from the hole (figure 3.10). For each ball, stand behind the ball and imagine the line to the hole. Place your putter perpendicular to the imaginary

3.10 Around-the-world drill.

line, directly behind the center of the ball. The object is to go "around the world" or around the hole and make all five or six putts in a row. This drill will help you develop your routine for aiming your putter with each putt starting from a different point.

TEE DRILL

Place a golf tee in the green. Position the ball five feet from the tee. The goal is to hit the tee. Having the target smaller will make the actual hole seem much larger. After hitting the tee 20 times, position yourself from the golf hole the same distance you were from the tee. Notice how much bigger the target looks! You should find putts to the hole easier to make.

PLAY THE GAME

Challenge a partner or yourself to a putting game of 18 holes. Use a scorecard to keep track of your score. Most courses will have at least 9 different holes cut in a practice green. Choose a starting point and move in a circle around the green, putting from each hole to the next using the hole last played as the new starting point. Write down a score after each ball is holed. Play 9 or 18 holes and add up your score. The object is to achieve two putts or fewer for each hole played. If you play 9 holes, a score of 18 or less would be excellent!

ACHIEVE AND PROCEED: PUTTING

- Develop a posture in putting that will allow your arms and shoulders to relax, and have your eyes lined up over the putting line.
- Use a pendulum stroke; hands, arms, and shoulders move together as one unit while the body remains still.
- The distance the putt rolls is determined by the length of the stroke.
- The direction of the ball is controlled by the alignment of the putter face and influenced by the slope of the green once the ball is in motion.
- Practice the stroke without using the target.
- Practice distance control to help eliminate three putting.
- Treat every putt as a "straight" putt.
- Putting accounts for 43 percent of the total strokes in a round of golf.

Chipping

A chip shot is an extension of the putting stroke. In building your golf swing, this is the logical progression to take. The chip shot is part of the *short game*, which is any part of the game that requires less than a full swing to execute the shot. Accurate chipping can lead to lower scores. A good short game also puts less pressure on the long game. Chipping is a smaller and simpler motion to execute than the longer swing used for pitch shots. Pitching, which will be discussed in chapter 5, is only necessary when you need to have the ball fly high into the air to travel over a sand bunker or larger amount of grass. Ideally you will chip anytime you can and pitch only when you have to!

A chip shot is used when the distance from the golf ball to the green is less than the distance from the edge of the green to the hole. The point of a chip shot is to land the ball on the first quarter of the green and allow it to roll to the hole like a putt. Rolling the ball up to the hole creates a greater chance of getting the ball near the hole or having the ball roll into the hole! The chip shot should have less time in the air and more time rolling on the ground like a putt.

Mastering the chipping game will give you the opportunity to get the ball up and down. In golf, *up and down* is when you chip the ball onto the green and take only one putt to put the ball in the hole. Once you master the chip shot, your chance for lower golf scores is much greater. You will have many more "up and downs." Strong chipping skills can fool your opponents into thinking they have you beat on a hole if they are the green and you are off the edge.

Chip It!

Think of the chip shot as an extension of the putting stroke. The same pendulum motion is used; only the body position is different. For a chip shot, the ball needs to get into the air to travel over a small amount of grass and then land on the green. Setting up to make a chip shot is very important to executing the shot correctly. The correct setup will enhance the proper motion. Set yourself up for success by placing your hands closer to the shaft of the club, down on the grip (figure 4.1). This will make the club shorter and easier to control. Placing your hands farther down on the grip does not give more power but more accuracy. In this type of shot we are not looking for power but control. The length of the club is not needed because this shot requires more finesse than power.

Narrow your stance and place your target foot back slightly. This is referred to as an *open stance*, which allows a better view of the target (figure 4.2). (This is very similar to the position used when tossing a ball underhand to a target.) Tip slightly forward from your hips with a slight bend in your legs. You may feel as if you are about to sit on a stool. Lean toward the target so that most of your weight remains on your target foot. Keeping your weight on your target foot ensures that the club will travel in a downward motion, which is necessary for making the ball "pop" up out of the grass. Your arms should

4.1 Proper hand position for the chip shot.

4.2 Open stance.

hang down from your shoulders, free of tension. Hint: Keep your grip light on the club and your hands close to your body; this will allow your arms to hang more freely.

The motion of the chipping swing is much like that of the putting stroke. Arms and shoulders should move together like a pendulum (figure 4.3). Keep the swing short to begin learning the motion. For a chip shot within 10 feet of the green, the distance of the swing will be about one foot back and one foot through. Shots farther from the green will require longer swings. However, you want to keep the back swing and forward swing equal to allow for proper rhythm and timing in the stroke. A common error is to make the back swing too long for the shot and the forward swing shorter, which causes the club to slow down before hitting the ball. This will result in a poor shot, one that does not allow the ball to reach the intended target.

To be your own coach, check to see how your follow-through looks by freezing in the finished position and asking yourself these questions: Is your weight on your target foot? Are your hands past your target leg? Is your clubface square to your target line? Did your club brush the grass in the center of your stance? Practice this skill before attempting it on an actual hole.

4.3a   Back swing.

4.3b   Forward swing.

Visualizing Swing Length Use the clock diagram in figure 4.4 to help visualize the length of your swing. For most chip shots within 10 feet of the green, the swing will move only from 7 o'clock to 5 o'clock. Other swings can then vary from a 7 to 5 o'clock swing, to an 8 to 4 o'clock swing, to a 9 to 3 o'clock swing, depending on the length of the shot needed.

4.4	Visualizing swing length.

Choosing a Club The chip shot is easier if you understand how to use the different clubs in your bag. You can choose to chip with only one of your irons, but you will have to alter your swing constantly to adjust to the various chipping distances. Club selection depends on the distance from the ball to the green and from the hole to the edge of the green. The idea is to land the ball on the green as soon as possible and roll the ball to the hole like a putt.

Use a variety of clubs from the same position and carefully observe the amount of distance the ball rolls with each club. A more lofted club such as the pitching wedge or 9 iron will cause the ball to roll less than a less lofted club such as the 6 or 5 iron. If you can learn the skill of the chip, you need only change the "tool" (club) in your hand to produce different distances with a swing of the same length. For example, if the ball lies 10 feet from the green and the hole is 15 feet from the edge of the green, use a pitching wedge to chip the ball (figure 4.5). The pitching wedge has a lot of loft and will cause the ball to fall onto the green at a steeper angle. This will

> **4.5** The ball lies 10 feet outside the green, and the hole is 15 feet in from the edge of the green. A pitching wedge is selected for the shot so that the ball rolls less.

cause the ball to slow down more quickly and produce less roll. The ball would land 3 feet onto the green and roll 12 feet to the hole. If the shot requires even less time for the ball to roll, use a sand wedge or lob wedge.

If the ball is 10 feet from the green and the hole is 30 feet from the edge of the green, you may choose to chip with a 7 iron rather than the pitching wedge you used for the 15-foot shot (figure 4.6). The swing would be the same length as used for the shorter shot. Because the 7 iron is not as lofted as the pitching wedge, the ball will not have as much height when it travels in the air. The ball will come onto the green with a shallower arc so there will be less to slow it down once it lands, allowing the ball to roll more.

Keep in mind that on chip shots farther from the green, you will need a more lofted club and a slightly longer swing to carry the longer grass before the green (figure 4.7). As long as the distance the ball needs to travel before getting to the green is less than the distance of green to the hole, you will use a chip shot. The club you select will make the difference in how high the ball will fly into the air and how much it will roll once it hits the green. More than 15 feet from the green usually requires the use of an 8 iron up to the pitching wedge to chip the ball.

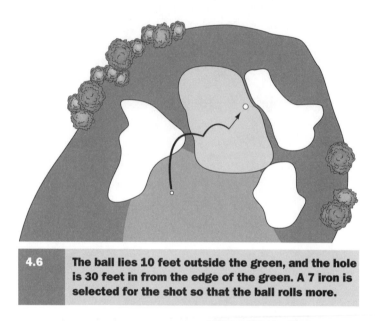

| 4.6 | The ball lies 10 feet outside the green, and the hole is 30 feet in from the edge of the green. A 7 iron is selected for the shot so that the ball rolls more. |

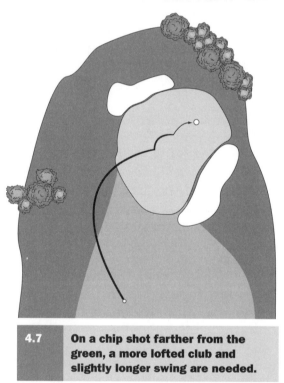

| 4.7 | On a chip shot farther from the green, a more lofted club and slightly longer swing are needed. |

Taking Aim   Chipping is very much like putting. You want to roll the ball to the hole instead of trying to lob it into the air so it lands next to the hole. Therefore, treat aiming the chip shot much like aiming a putt. Look at the slope of the green to the hole from where your ball is located. If the green is higher on the left side of the hole, the ball will tend to roll down to the right of the hole. Therefore you need to aim to the left of the hole, not at the hole directly. Walk up on the green to the hole to take a proper view of how the green slopes around the hole. Picture the line the ball will take when it hits the surface of the green. Gravity will cause the ball to roll down the hills. Choose a spot to hit the ball to and trust your decision.

When aiming your clubface, use the bottom edge of the club to form a perpendicular angle to your imaginary target line (figure 4.8). Take into account the best putting location once the ball is on the green. An uphill putt is always easier to control than a downhill putt. In a downhill putt the ball may miss the hole and pick up speed as it passes the hole, leaving your next putt possibly longer than the first one. Planning ahead for the next shot can save you strokes and frustration. Be sure to know where the uphill putt is when making your decision to chip. All players guess to some extent, but experience will make you a better guesser. As you play more and have more opportunities to chip the ball onto the green, you will gain more confidence. Remember, this is where you can lower your scores!

4.8   **The clubface forms a perpendicular angle to the imaginary target line.**

Chip or Putt?

Chipping can be easy, but is often overlooked by many recreational players. Many golfers waste shots around the green because they have not worked on chipping. Knowing what type of shot to hit and what club to use is a big part of the game. The correct decision can make a two- or three-stroke difference.

When the ball is near the green, the first question you should ask yourself is, Can I putt it? You may want to putt the ball if the grass between the ball and the green is closely mown and fairly flat. The reason is simple: The putt is the simplest golf shot. There is less error when all that is required is to roll the ball along the ground. If putting is not an option, the next question you should ask yourself is, Can I chip it? Chip the ball whenever the distance of green to the golf hole is greater than the distance of the fairway to the green. Analyze the ratio between these distances before choosing a club.

Next examine the surface of the green. Does the green slope uphill or downhill to the hole? A green that is sloping uphill to the hole may require a less lofted club for the particular shot. A green that is sloping downhill may require a club with more loft to keep the ball from rolling too far past the hole. In both cases your goal should be to chip the ball just under the hole to give yourself an uphill putt. Chipping a ball past the hole when the slope is uphill can make the next shot very difficult.

Think ahead to the next shot when making your decision about where to chip to and what club you should use. Is the green fast or slow, wet or dry? Usually a wet green will slow the ball down and a dry green will speed it up. In the case of a wet green, you may want to use a less lofted club to allow the ball to roll to the hole. A dry green is typically much faster in speed and may need a more lofted club to keep the ball from rolling past the hole.

If the length of the shot looks like it requires an 8 iron but the green slopes uphill, you may want to choose a 7 iron, which will allow the ball to roll more. Conversely, if the green slopes downhill, you may want to use a 9 iron. The idea is to change the club and keep the same swing motion. This makes the shot easier because you will not have to adjust the length of the swing. Simply trust the club you have selected to do the job for you!

Drills and games are perfect ways to enhance your knowledge of and feel for the chip shot. Because many different clubs can be used for chipping, experiment with all of your irons.

STORK DRILL

The stork drill will help you master the proper motion. Set up with the proper posture to the ball for chipping. Place your trail foot behind you, resting on the toe, so you have all your weight on your target foot (figure 4.9). This will keep your weight where it needs to be and allow the club to work in a downward motion. Swing your shoulders and arms in a pendulum motion, keeping all your weight on the target foot. Your club should clip the grass at the bottom of your swing. Practice this drill with and without a golf ball.

4.9 Stork drill.

SHAFT TO TARGET ARM

The shaft to target arm drill will help establish the proper arm motion. This drill is helpful if you have trouble using too much hand and not enough arm swing during the shot. Hold the grip down toward the shaft with your target hand. Place the shaft up against your target arm as if you were putting a splint on your arm (figure 4.10). Stand with the correct posture, weight and hands toward the target. Make a small swinging motion using the shoulders first to make the arms swing. The shaft of the club should remain up against your target arm if done correctly. Repeat until you are able to keep your hands still and move the club like a pendulum with your arms.

4.10 **Shaft-to-target-arm drill.**

TOWEL-TO-TOWEL EXERCISE

The towel-to-towel exercise will help establish a picture of how the shot should be executed. Place a golf towel three feet onto the green and another towel next to the hole or just under the hole if it is an uphill chip (figure 4.11). (Remember, you want to plan for the easy putt. Uphill putts are much easier to make.) The idea is to land the ball on the center of the closest towel and allow the ball to roll onto the second towel near the hole. By giving you larger targets, this drill lessens the stress by allowing room for error. Set up towels to different targets so you can practice with different clubs. You also can

4.11 Towel-to-towel exercise.

step back from the green, using the same spots for the towels but a different club. As you move away from the green, use a more lofted club. For example, if you were using a 7 iron 5 feet from the green, use an 8 iron 10 feet from the green but still aim at the first towel and allow the ball to roll to the second towel. Work toward getting at least 60 percent of your shots to hit both towels.

THREE-CLUB DRILL

The three-club drill will help you understand the ways different clubs affect the golf ball in the chip shot. Take your 5, 7, and 9 irons or a pitching wedge, 8 iron, and 6 iron. Drop three golf balls just off the green. Hit one ball with each club. Notice the amount of roll each ball has. Be sure your swings are the same length and hit the balls just onto the surface of the green. Repeat as needed to achieve a better understanding of the clubs and how they are different.

BUDDY UP-AND-DOWN

The buddy up-and-down game creates a gamelike situation to help you apply your chipping skills during a game. This is a fun activity for an even number of players (minimum of four). First set up a course of 9 or 18 holes around a practice green. Choose the starting point by using small tees near the green to establish where each shot should be played and which hole the shot should aim toward. Each team consists of two players. For the first 9 holes, one player chips the ball to the green and the other finishes the hole by putting the ball to the appropriate hole. A score is recorded after each hole. You may use a regular golf scorecard to keep track of the team score. Set par at 2 or 3 depending on the skill level of the group. After 9 holes, the "chipper" becomes the "putter" and the "putter" becomes the "chipper." At the conclusion of 18 holes, the scores are added. The team with the lowest score wins! The game works well for both large and small groups as long as the holes are well marked. If you are practicing alone, modify the game by being both the chipper and the putter. Play 9 or 18 holes and keep score. Try to improve your score or count your "up and down" percentage.

ACHIEVE AND PROCEED: CHIPPING

- Place your hands down on the grip to shorten the club.
- Open your stance by placing your target foot back.

- Tilt forward as if you are sitting on a stool.
- Have your hands and weight toward the target side.
- Move the club with your shoulders and arms like a pendulum.
- Use different clubs to control distance with each shot.
- The length of swing will increase as you are farther from the green.
- The surface of the green is important in determining the shot and club used.
- Improve your score by improving the number of times you get the ball "up and down."

5

CHAPTER

Pitch Shots

As soon as you begin to move farther from the green and the distance to the green is greater than the distance from the edge of the putting green to the hole, you will need to consider pitching the ball instead of chipping it. Like the chip shot, the pitch shot is used to approach the green. The pitch shot is considered part of the short game, which makes up 63 percent of the shots taken in a round of golf. The pitch shot is used when you must elevate the ball over a large amount of grass or up and over a sand bunker, water hazard, or possibly even a small tree next to a green. Because the pitch shot allows the ball to travel higher in the air than the chip shot, the ball will have less roll on the green once it lands.

Pitch swings vary in length depending on the distance needed to carry the ball. Club selection may also vary depending on the number of wedges you have in your set. The clubs used for pitching include a pitching wedge, a sand wedge, or any lob wedge. A lob wedge has more loft than the pitching or sand wedge, thus allowing the ball to travel even higher in the air and creating a softer landing. For some pitch shots, you may elect to land the ball just on the fringe of the green and have it bounce to the hole. This type of shot is referred to as a *pitch and run*. In a typical pitch shot, the goal is to land the ball half the distance to the hole with little roll once the ball lands.

Pitch It!

If you can throw water out of a bucket or toss a ball underhand, you can execute the pitch shot. Most pitch shots are executed with a pitching wedge, sand wedge, or lob wedge and require less than a full swing.

Beginning with the correct setup position is most important. The setup for the pitch is similar to that for the chip. Tilt forward from your hips, keeping your back in a straight line with the back of your head (figure 5.1a). Place your target foot back toward the heel of your trail foot to assume a more open stance. Position your feet approximately a foot apart with a slight flex to your legs (figure 5.1b). Too much knee bend is not good and will keep you from shifting your weight properly. Your weight should be evenly distributed. The ball position in the pitch shot is center to just slightly toward the target foot depending on the amount of height you want. If you need the ball to move up in the air quickly because of an obstacle, then move the ball closer to the target foot.

Unlike the putting stroke or chip swing, the pitch swing is a two-lever motion that requires a slight fold to the trail arm in the back swing. The folding of the trail arm allows the wrists to hinge and the club to travel up (figure 5.1c). The arms will travel to at least the 9 o'clock position using the clock method described in chapter 4. The weight will transfer to the inside of the trail foot on longer pitch shots. Shorter pitch shots (under 30 yards from the green) can be played with most of the weight remaining on the target foot.

Begin the forward motion by turning your hips toward the target and shifting your weight to your target foot (figure 5.1d). Because you

| 5.1a | Setup for the shot. |

| 5.1b | Feet are in position. |

are farther from the target, you need more clubhead speed to send the ball a greater distance. The clubhead will swing faster if you use your lower body. Just as in throwing, when your arm swings back, you conserve energy on your back foot. When you move your weight to your target foot, your arm will swing forward with greater speed. You conserve your energy in the back swing and you expend the energy toward the target in the forward swing. Keep your head from moving as you turn through to the target. Your head will rotate up to see the shot but shouldn't move before hitting the ball.

This same concept is used for throwing a ball or swinging a tennis racket. A similar movement is used in most sports that require an object to get from one point to another. As your weight shifts from the back foot to the front foot, keep your head steady. The arm position in the forward swing resembles the arm position that would be used when throwing a ball underhand. The palm of the trail hand is turned toward the sky when the swing is completed.

As with all golf shots, maintaining good rhythm and balance is important. Practice the motion without using a golf ball. When you have a sense of the swing, place a ball at the center of your stance. Make a very short swing that requires only a very small amount of weight shift. The loft of the club will send the ball farther into the air as long as the club moves down and through the ball. Do not try to help the ball go into the air in any way. As you turn toward the target and your club moves down toward the ground, the ball will ascend into the air. Swing down and the ball goes up!

| 5.1c | Back swing. |

| 5.1d | Forward swing. |

The pitch shot has many variations because it can be used from several distances and in many circumstances, such as having to loft the ball over an obstacle. The simplest form of the pitch shot is to use any wedge and execute the swing like the chip shot. This means keeping your weight on your target foot throughout the swing. Swing the club the same distance back and through. Swing length varies depending on the distance the ball needs to travel.

Again, just as you would when playing catch with a friend, as you move farther away from your target, your arm swing length increases. The only difference with the pitch shot is that you have a club in your hand. Imagine a clock. If you swing back to 8 o'clock, you should swing through to 4 o'clock (figure 5.2). If you swing back to 9 o'clock, you should swing through to 3 o'clock, and so on.

Decide for yourself when you need more power in your swing to make the ball travel the distance to the green. When more energy is required, simply shift your weight from your back foot to your front foot and make the swing longer.

5.2 If your back swing goes to 8 o'clock, your forward swing should go to 4 o'clock.

Pitch and Run The pitch and run is used when there is a smooth surface of fairway just before the green or there is a large amount of green before the hole. Because this shot is easier to execute than a lofted pitch shot that would make the ball stop on the green with little roll, choose the pitch and run if you can. To execute the pitch and run, address the ball with a slightly open stance, play the ball in the center of your stance, and allow the arms to rotate through the swing. The toe of the club will point to the sky at the end of the forward swing. Again, you may vary the length of the shot depending on the distance the ball needs to travel. A pitching wedge is the club of choice because it has less loft than other wedges, which will allow for more roll.

Pitch Over an Obstacle   The pitch or lob shot is necessary when a bunker, water hazard, or small tree appears between the ball and the green. The pitch or lob shot will carry the ball higher into the air, which allows it to land on the green with little roll. For this shot, use a more lofted wedge such as a sand wedge or lob wedge. The sand wedge will typically have 52 degrees of loft, whereas a lob wedge will have 56 to 60 degrees of loft. The more degrees of loft, the higher the ball can travel. The ball should be positioned inside the target foot, allowing it to take off higher from the start of the shot. When the ball flies higher into the air, more air can get under the ball, which produces more spin and keeps the ball from rolling once it hits the green.

When pitching over a obstacle, the swing is a two-lever motion. The trail arm bends, allowing the club to travel higher in the back swing. In the forward swing, the lower body shifts to the target foot and the hands and arms travel down and through with the clubface remaining turned to the sky. (Note: the palm of the trail hand also faces the sky as in an underhanded ball toss.) This produces more backspin on the ball and will cause the shot to land "softer." The swing length will be no less than 9 to 3 o'clock.

Take it to the course

Good Choices

When the ball lies close to the green, making the right choice is imperative to lower scores. Know when to pitch and run and when to pitch. Keep in mind that the pitch and run is the easier shot to execute, particularly under pressure. As long as the hole is toward the center or back of the green and you have only fairway between the ball and the green, choose the pitch and run. For a pitch and run, choose a 9 iron or pitching wedge. Remember that less lofted clubs allow the ball to fly lower and roll farther.

If the hole is located near the edge of the green or your ball lies behind a sand bunker, pitch the ball using a sand wedge or lob wedge.

Because there is little time for the ball to roll once it hits the green, a higher shot to allow the ball to land with less roll is required. Swing length depends on the distance you need to carry to get the ball to the green. Swing length also varies depending on the type of wedge you use. A higher lofted wedge will require a longer swing. The ball will travel higher and shorter with a more lofted wedge.

The terrain the ball lies on also is a factor when choosing the club and type of pitch shot. If the ball is on an uphill lie, choose to pitch with the 9 iron or pitching wedge instead of a lob wedge. When your club sits on an uphill lie, the loft increases. A common mistake many golfers make is to use a high lofted club on an uphill lie. The ball tends to come up short of the target because of the higher loft created by the slope. Use the 9 iron or pitching wedge with the same swing you would take if you were hitting the shot with your lob wedge. The slope simply turns the pitching wedge into the same amount of loft as the lob wedge. Conversely, if the ball lies on a downhill slope, a more lofted club such as a sand or lob wedge would be appropriate because the downhill slope will take loft off the club. When you are setting up to a ball on an uneven slope, be sure to position your body with the slope. On an uphill lie your shoulders should run parallel with the slope, allowing the club to swing along the hill.

Give it a go

Sixty-three percent of the shots taken in a round of golf require less than a full swing. In other words, over half of your shots will be putts, chips, or pitches. It only makes sense to spend at least half of your time practicing and fine-tuning these skills to achieve lower golf scores. In the game of golf, you have only one try at a particular target. Practicing from different distances and with different targets will better prepare you for the variations that arise in the game itself. Most important, however, is to have fun while learning. Practice alone or with a friend, but remember to keep it fun.

UNDERHAND BALL TOSS

Take a tennis ball or any ball that fits comfortably in your hand. Stand similar to the way you would set up for the pitch shot (figure 5.3a). Toss the ball underhand. Notice how the ball travels up in the air and straight ahead. Be sure to turn and face your target. If

5.3a-b Underhand ball toss drill.

the palm of your trail hand is turned up to the sky, you are facing the target, and most of your weight is on your target foot, you have executed the drill correctly (figure 5.3b).

BUCKET DRILL

Use a range ball bucket or any plastic bucket. Hold the top of the bucket with your target hand and place your trail hand at the bottom of the bucket. Pretend you have a full bucket of water. The object is to toss the water out of the bucket to a target in front of you. Set up your position as you would for the pitch shot (figure 5.4). Swing the bucket back and through and freeze in the follow-through position. The back of your target hand should be turned to the sky, and the palm of your trail hand should face the sky. The opening in the bucket should face the target.

5.4 **Bucket drill.**

TRAIL ARM PRACTICE

Hold the club down on the grip toward the shaft with your trail hand. Place your target hand on your trail arm just where the arm will fold. Position your body using an open stance as if you were about to execute a pitch shot. Swing the club back using only the trail arm. The trail arm should fold in the back swing. You should be able to feel the arm folding with your target hand. In the forward swing, allow your weight to shift to your target foot. The club will swing to the ground as you feel your trail arm staying close to your side on the follow-through. The clubface should face up to the sky. The palm of your trail hand is therefore also facing up to the sky, just as it would in the underhand ball toss.

TOE-UP TO TOE-UP

This drill is for practicing the pitch and run. Set up in the proper posture and swing the club halfway back (approximately to 9 o'clock) with the toe of the club turned to the sky. Complete the forward swing by shifting your weight to your target foot and swing the club to the 3 o'clock position with the toe of the club facing the sky. Your arms should rotate through the swing, allowing the toe of the club to finish pointed toward the sky.

BEACH TOWEL DRILL

This is a more practical drill to practice the shot using a target. (The mechanics of the swing should be practiced first.) Place a beach towel halfway to the hole on the green. Place another beach towel next to the hole or just over the hole. Step off 20, 30, and 40 yards. Place three balls at the 20-yard distance, three balls at the 30-yard distance, and three balls at the 40-yard distance. Pitch the balls so they land on the first beach towel. The goal is to have the balls roll a short distance to the second towel located near the hole. If you can get two out of the three balls to roll to the second towel, you are doing great!

AROUND THE WORLD

Scatter 20 or 30 balls around a green in various places and distances from the green. Be sure to have a variety of clubs—9 iron, pitching wedge, sand wedge, and lob wedge. Analyze each shot to determine the best club choice and type of pitch to use. Keep track of how many balls you pitch within 10 feet of the hole. Making the correct choice around the green is just as essential to scoring as executing the proper swing motion. Remember, the more loft a club has, the higher the ball will travel and the shorter amount of roll it will have once it hits the green.

ACHIEVE AND PROCEED: PITCH SHOTS

- Pitch shots are made using the wedges: pitching, sand, and lob.
- Use an open stance with pitch shots.

- Pitching requires a two-lever swing.
- Short pitch shots keep more weight on the target foot.
- Longer pitch shots shift the weight to generate more clubhead speed.
- Pitch and run shots require a rotation in the arms to allow the ball to roll more once it lands on the green.
- Pitch shots that require the ball to travel high and have little roll will usually be made with the sand or lob wedge.
- When around the green, chip when you can and pitch when you have to.

6

Bunker Shots

Sand bunkers were a natural part of the landscape in Scotland where the game of golf originated. The sheep would bury themselves in the banks to protect themselves from the cold coastal winds, causing the grass to wear away and forming sandy areas. Sand bunkers help to define the shapes of the fairways, greens, and holes. Most players refer to courses without bunkers or water hazards as "cow pastures." As you play the game, you will find yourself in a bunker at one time or another.

In the design of most golf courses there are fairway bunkers and greenside bunkers, or hazards. Fairway bunkers are located along the golf hole left or right or across the fairway. Greenside bunkers are located in front of, to the left or right side of, or behind the green. In the rules of golf you are not allowed to *ground* your club in a hazard before your shot. Grounding your club means setting your club down so that it touches the surface of the hazard. The penalty for grounding your club is two strokes. For example, if you lie three in a bunker and you ground your club prior to hitting the shot, you incur a two-stroke penalty. You are now lying six.

A fairway bunker shot is hit like a shot off the fairway with a few exceptions. A greenside bunker shot requires more swing than a chip or pitch because the sand slows the club down. The idea is to swing the club through the sand. The sand gets between the clubface and the ball, and as the club accelerates through the sand, it forces the sand to carry the ball out of the bunker. Displacing the right amount of sand and understanding the difference between clubface position and ball position will allow you to hit all the various shots you may encounter in a sand bunker.

Escape the Sand

To properly execute bunker shots, you first need to understand the design of the sand wedge. The sand wedge is more lofted than the pitching wedge. It also has a wider sole or bottom, a design feature called a

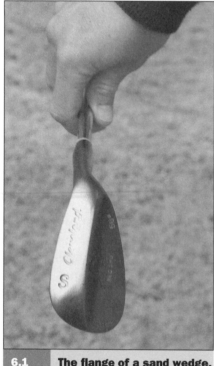

The flange of a sand wedge.

flange (figure 6.1). The flange of the club is meant to provide *bounce*. This bounce provided by the flange allows the club to glide through and on top of the sand rather than dig into the sand. To picture the purpose of the design of the sand wedge, think of a ski. The tip of a ski curves up to keep it from digging into the snow or water. The tip of the ski enables the ski to glide over the snow or water. Place the clubhead of the sand wedge on your hand and rotate it to the right if you are right-handed or to the left if you are left-handed. Notice how the front edge of the club resembles a ski after you have rotated the club. The design of the sand wedge keeps the club from digging into the sand.

Open the face of the club; then grip your sand wedge and walk into the sand. Use your feet to feel how much sand you have under the ball. The more sand you have to work with, the more you may want to turn or rotate the face of your club to an open position. If the clubface is square, the leading edge of the clubhead will tend to dig into the sand. Your club will go into the sand deeper than desired, which will slow down the speed of the club, leaving the ball in the sand. Your feet should be open to the target line, and your shoulders should be parallel to the target line (figure 6.2a). The ball should be closer to the target foot. This is referred to as *up in the stance.*

When setting up to hit the sand shot, hold the club above the sand two to three inches behind the ball. The club should enter the sand prior to the ball. To envision the amount of sand displaced in a sand shot, picture a dollar bill with the ball in the center of the bill. The amount of sand displaced is represented by the amount of the dollar bill on either side of the ball. The club will move through the sand and displace the sand on both sides of the ball. Approximately six to seven inches of sand is displaced in a greenside bunker shot. Holding the club above the sand will keep you from grounding your club in the hazard.

The basic swing of a greenside bunker shot is similar to that of a pitch shot. The shoulders turn as the arms swing back and the trail arm bends slightly as the club moves up (figure 6.2b). The forward swing begins with the body turning through to the target as the arms move down and through (figure 6.2c). The target arm needs to pull through to keep the trail hand from taking over and flipping the clubhead in front of the hands. This is a common error that leads to the ball remaining in the sand or hitting only the ball rather than the sand, sending it over the green.

Note that a club moving through sand will encounter resistance much like your hand will when moving through water. A longer swing is needed to give the club more acceleration as it moves through the sand. The length of the swing for a greenside bunker will generally be at least 9 to 3 o'clock and usually closer to 10 to 2 o'clock. When you complete a bunker shot, the clubface will point to the sky, your body will face the target, and more of your balance will be on your target foot. The club will enter the sand a good inch to inch and a half behind the ball and carry through the same distance to the other side, similar to the size of a dollar bill.

| 6.2a | Preparing the setup. |

| 6.2b | Back swing for the bunker shot. |

| 6.2c | Forward swing for the bunker shot. |

Ideally, a ball that lands in a greenside bunker will rest on top of the sand and close to the green. When this occurs, use the technique explained in You Can Do It. Most bunkers next to a green require the use of a sand wedge. The sand wedge is the best choice whenever you have to blast through the sand to get the ball out of the bunker. One consideration is how close the ball is to the front of the bunker, which is sometimes referred to as the *lip* of the bunker. The lip of the bunker can vary in height. If there is very little lip to the bunker, you may be able to putt the ball out of the bunker. Most greenside bunkers have a lip that requires the ball to get up in the air to travel over.

Two types of swing shapes are used in a greenside bunker shot: a V-shaped swing and a U-shaped swing. A V-shaped swing is used when the lie of the ball is close to the lip of the bunker, which usually requires the ball to travel high quickly. Visualize the difference in the swing shapes by picturing bouncing a ball on the floor. If you bounce the ball straight down, it will bounce back straight up. If you bounce the ball at a 45-degree angle, it would move up at a 45-degree angle.

A V-shaped swing is used more for shorter bunker shots. For the short bunker shot, bring your hands farther down the grip to make the club shorter. This gives you more control of the club when the length of the shaft is not needed. To create more of a V-shaped swing, position the ball closer to your target foot and put most of your weight on your target foot. Your shoulders will turn as your arms come up in a more vertical plane. The sharper angle of the club in the back swing will allow the club to return at the steeper angle, allowing the ball to elevate quickly out of the bunker. The V-shaped swing is used for shorter shots because the higher trajectory will allow for less roll when the ball lands on the green.

A U-shaped swing is used more for shots that need to travel over more sand or more green before reaching the target. It is similar to bouncing a ball on the floor at a 45-degree angle. For this shot position the ball more to the center of the stance with your weight more evenly distributed. Your shoulders will turn as your arms come back at a shallow arc to the sand. Turn your body through and the club will return to the sand with a shallow arc, allowing the ball to come out of the sand with a lower trajectory and cover more distance.

Playing a Bad Lie   Golf is played under many different circumstances that can affect the lie of the ball. A ball that is buried in the sand or a ball that has very little sand underneath it is considered to be in a bad lie. To play a bad lie, stand with the ball closer to the back of your stance or toward your trail foot (figure 6.3). To remember where to play the ball, think "bad lie, play back" or "bad back." This is opposite of where you should stand if the ball is up on the sand. Square the clubface by leaving the leading edge perpendicular to the target line. Remember that we opened the clubface with a sand shot to allow the flange to enter the sand first. In this situation there is little sand to move the club through. The flange would bounce off the hard surface or slide over the buried lie. By keeping the leading edge of the clubface square, we can create a "digging tool" rather than a snow ski. A digging tool is needed to move the club into the sand. In a buried lie in which the ball is under the sand, the club needs to move farther into the sand

6.3 **To play a bad lie, stand so the ball is toward your trail foot.**

to help elevate the ball out. In a lie with little sand under the ball, the leading edge is used to pitch the ball off the surface of the sand and onto the green.

Playing a Fairway Bunker   A fairway bunker is much farther from the green than a greenside bunker. Fairway bunkers typically appear beside a fairway or intersect across a fairway. Playing a fairway bunker is more like playing off the grass than playing out of a greenside bunker. Fairway bunkers have a shallower layer of sand and generally a lower lip at the front.

To play a fairway bunker, you first must choose a club that will lift the ball to the appropriate height to clear the lip of the bunker. To get a sense of how high the ball will go if struck off a particular club, lay the club on the ground with the face of the club pointing toward the sky and gently step on the clubface. The shaft of the club will rise into the air. This demonstrates approximately how high the ball will go if struck properly on the clubface. New golfers should do this with all the irons to learn how the ball reacts to different lofts.

Choose a club that will lift the ball over the lip and give you the best chance of advancing close to the target. Almost any club can be used in a fairway bunker as long as it is appropriate for the conditions. Choose a club based on the height the ball needs to achieve to fly over the front of the bunker and toward the target. The club choice for most fairway shots is a 5 to 7 iron. Some lofted woods may be used, such as a 7 or 9, if the sand conditions are firm and the lip of the bunker is not very high.

Once you have chosen a club, you are ready to set up to the ball. Play the ball in the center of your stance and assume a proper posture by tilting forward from your hips. Dig your feet into the sand to keep from slipping during the swing. Take less than a full swing to maintain balance and ensure proper contact (figure 6.4).

Your goal is to get the ball out of the bunker and back in play. Give yourself the opportunity to do so by following these rules: First, choose the appropriate club to clear the lip. Second, use a three-quarter swing to maintain balance and control. Third, swing through the ball as you would on the fairway. You will brush the sand slightly, unlike in a greenside bunker shot in which you want to explode through the sand. The total amount of sand taken is three to four inches, which is half of what is taken in a greenside bunker.

6.4 **Escaping a fairway bunker.**

The Unplayable Lie

Golf has several rules specific to playing from sand bunkers. As mentioned earlier, grounding your club in the sand prior to hitting a bunker shot will result in a two-stroke penalty. Another infraction that results in a two-stroke penalty is moving anything in a bunker that is considered a natural part of the golf course, such as sticks, leaves, stones, or pinecones. Man-made objects such as rakes, which are often found in bunkers, may be removed. Proper etiquette after playing a bunker shot requires you to rake any footprints or displacement of sand so that you leave the bunker in better shape than you found it.

Sometimes a ball may be in a difficult position in a bunker. The player is the sole judge as to whether the ball is playable according to the player's skill level. For example, the ball may be lodged in the lip of a bunker. More skilled players may choose to advance the ball. Other players, however, may find the shot impossible, therefore choosing to take an *unplayable lie*.

In the rules of golf you have three options when taking an unplayable lie. However, in a sand bunker you have only two options. The first option is to measure two club lengths (using any club) from the ball without going closer to the hole and still being in the bunker. Drop the ball with your arm held out at shoulder height, within the measured distance of the two club lengths. If the ball rolls closer to the hole, you should drop again. If it rolls closer to the hole on the second drop, you must place it where it first touched the sand. The second unplayable lie option is to go back where the last shot was played from before going into the bunker. Drop the ball as near as possible to the spot determined by you and your playing competitors and proceed to play out the hole. In either case, when you lift a ball to take an unplayable lie, you must count a penalty of one stroke to your total score for the hole. If you lay two in the bunker and took an unplayable lie under penalty of one stroke, you would then be hitting your fourth shot.

EGG EXERCISE

Place a ball on top of the sand. Draw a circle about four inches in diameter around the ball. The ball is the yoke and the circle is the white of the egg (figure 6.5). The idea is to remove the circle of sand without concern for the ball. In other words, flip the egg over easy

6.5 | Egg exercise.

without breaking the yoke. The egg white is all that matters. Get into a greenside bunker stance—open stance and open clubface—and swing through the circle, flipping the egg out of the bunker by moving the club through the entire circle. If the circle lines are still showing in the sand, you probably caught only the yoke or ball. You may want to practice just drawing circles about four inches in diameter and swinging your club through the sand to make the circle disappear before adding the ball.

BOARD DRILL

This drill will exaggerate the feel for the different ways the club can move through the sand. As discussed earlier, a sand wedge can be used as a snow ski or a digging tool depending on the lie of the ball in the sand. Bury a block of wood approximately one foot long just under the sand. Place about two inches of sand on the board. Practice swinging your club with the face open over the board. Try to feel the bounce of the club as it moves through the sand rather than digging too deeply into the sand. The bounce effect comes from the flange hitting the board. Then place only one inch of sand on the board. Practice swinging your club with the face of the club square to the target line. Keep the leading edge of the clubface perpendicular to the target line to use as a digging tool. This is needed for bad lies.

DOLLAR BILL DRILL

Place a dollar bill on top of the sand. You may need to use a little sand to weigh down the edges of the bill so it lies flat. Place the ball on George Washington's face (figure 6.6). Remember that the dollar bill is the same size as the amount of sand you want to displace. The club should enter the sand at the back of the bill and leave the sand at the front of the bill. The object is to keep the dollar bill whole, which is why I don't suggest using a 20!

6.6 **Dollar bill drill.**

ACHIEVE AND PROCEED: BUNKER SHOTS

- Recognize and understand the design of the sand wedge and how the design affects the shot.
- Know when to use the flange of the club as a leading edge, or ski, and when to use it as a digging tool.
- Use a V-shaped swing for short shots and a U-shaped swing for longer shots.
- Fairway bunker shots are much the same as playing shots off the fairway.
- Be sure to swing through the sand.
- Play fairway bunker shots like fairway shots, except make your club selection based on the lip of the bunker.

- Know the procedure for unplayable lies in the bunker.
- Be sure to rake the bunker after you have completed your shot.

Full Swing Fundamentals

In a full golf swing the nonmoving parts are more important than the moving parts. In other words, how you get ready to make a swing is more important than the swing itself. Without a proper setup position, you will have a hard time maintaining your balance throughout the swing. Without the proper placement of your hands on the club, you will have difficulty making the correct contact between the face of the club and the ball. Without properly aligning yourself to the intended target, your ball will not likely end up in an appropriate place.

To learn the full swing, begin by focusing your full attention on learning the preswing fundamentals. The preswing fundamentals include posture, grip, and alignment. The proper setup will make the movement of the golf swing easier. An incorrect setup will lead to problems in the swing that can be difficult to correct if they become habits. Be patient when learning the full swing fundamentals. Practice each fundamental one at a time, giving your full attention to each repetition. Habits are formed by repeating a task over and over again with full attention on what you want to learn. Once you have made habits of the preswing fundamentals, you are ready to move on to the moving parts of the swing.

Posture and Alignment

The three preswing fundamentals include posture, alignment, and grip. Grip, the third preswing fundamental, will be discussed in More to Choose and Use. Body position is the first preswing fundamental critical to the golf swing. Proper posture will create a better turning motion and more balance during the swing. A better turning motion and more balance will provide better ball contact and more consistency with the swing. This will also affect how far you will be able to hit the ball. In the proper posture the spine tilts forward from the hips, the back of the head is in line with the spine, the legs are slightly flexed, the weight is distributed equally on both the target and trail side but more to the balls of the feet, and the arms hang down from the shoulders.

The first concern of proper posture is the position of the feet. Place your feet shoulder-width apart by lining your underarms up with the insides of your feet. This will give you a solid base from which to swing and will also help your balance. To find the correct position of your spine, stand tall and keep the back of your head in line with your spine. Arms are loose and hanging by your side. Legs are locked. Now, place your hands on your hips just below your waistline. Tilt forward until your tailbone moves out. The back of your head, your spine, and your tailbone should all be in a line. Drop your arms and slightly flex your legs. Your arms will hang down from your shoulders, putting your hands approximately one handwidth away from your body (figure 7.1). Flex your legs only to the point at which your weight is on the balls of your feet. Keep your chin up and away from your body to allow for proper shoulder turn.

7.1 Proper posture.

This posture is sometimes referred to as the *athletic position.* When you go through the steps for proper posture, start without having a club in your hand. As you tilt forward and flex your legs slightly, think about what other sports you may be able to play in this position. You should feel as though you could jump straight up or move side to side quickly. If this is difficult, chances are good that you have bent over too much or that you are leaning back on your heels. The golfing posture is very similar to that of many athletic activities. Proper posture is easy to achieve. The real test is being able to stay in this position while making the full swing.

Alignment is the second preswing fundamental. Having the proper hand position and body position is important to making the swing motion, but neither fundamental will help if you are not aligned properly to the intended target. The first step to proper alignment is to identify the target line, the imaginary line that runs between the ball and the target. Stand directly behind the ball in relation to the target to find the target line. Identify a point or spot on the ground that falls on the target line within 10 feet of the ball. This is referred

to as an intermediate target. Position the clubface so the leading edge of the club is perpendicular to the target line. Once you have established the target line, you can establish the line for your body. Your body should simply be on a line parallel to the target line. In a proper setup, the club-face is lined up directly at the target and the body is parallel left of the target (figure 7.2).

7.2 **Proper alignment.**

The third preswing fundamental is grip. The hands are the golfer's only connection to the club. As such, they must be positioned to deliver the face of the club to the ball properly as well as to create the proper position for the club throughout the swing. Before learning the proper grip for a full swing, you should be able to identify the leading edge of the clubface. The bottom line of the clubhead is the leading edge. When the club is set behind the ball, the leading edge should be perpendicular to the target line.

Before gripping the club, let your arms hang relaxed by your sides with your palms facing in toward your body. Place the club in your target hand by dropping it from your trail hand into the fingers of your target hand with your target arm still hanging relaxed by your side. Close your hand on the grip of the club. Bring the club in front of your body and look at your hand position. Your thumb should be slightly off to the trail side of the grip while the pad of your palm rests on the top of the grip. The club is held in the fingers of the hand. To ensure the proper position of your target hand, hold the club in front of you using only your index finger and pad of your hand. Another check would be to place the club on the ground in front of you while holding it in your target hand. Turn the club to make a 90-degree angle with your target arm and the club shaft. Now lift the club to a 45-degree angle. Place the fingers of your trail hand on the club and connect your hands, using the pinky of your trail hand and the index finger of your target hand. The pinky of your trail hand lies between the index and second fingers of your target hand. Your trail hand should cover your target thumb, and your trail thumb should be slightly over to the target side of the grip (figure 7.3).

The hands are the golfer's connection to the club and directly influence the position of the face of the club. When holding the club, you should feel the pressure more in the middle two fingers of your target hand and last three fingers

7.3 Add the trail hand and overlap the fingers.

76

of your trail hand. Pressure applied with the index fingers and thumbs will cause the arms to tighten during the swing motion.

Once you are on the course, full swing fundamentals should be a habit. The variations in grip, posture, and alignment come into play when course conditions and weather call for slight adjustments. If the ball is not moving to the desired target, it may be due to a problem with alignment. If the ball is spinning in the air offline, your grip may need to be adjusted. If you are having difficulty making proper contact with the ball, it may be that your posture changes during the swing. Practice these fundamentals away from the course.

Alternative Grips   Grips may vary depending on the preference of the individual as well as the strength or size of the hands. Those with smaller hands may choose an overlapping grip (figure 7.4) rather than an interlocking grip. The difference is in the connection of the hands. Take the pinky finger of your trail hand and place it between the index finger and second finger of your target hand. This is referred to as an *interlocking grip*. The rest of the hand position on the club remains the same as explained in the beginning of this chapter.

The 10-finger grip (figure 7.5) is used more by junior players or players with very small hands. The club is still placed in the fingers of the hands but there is no connection between the two hands. The hands are placed on the club so they touch each other without overlapping or interlocking.

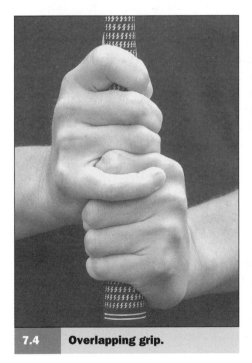

7.4   **Overlapping grip.**

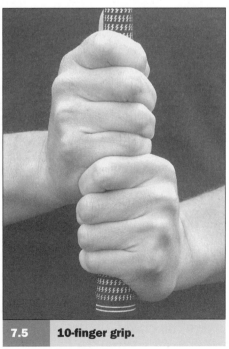

7.5   **10-finger grip.**

Grip strengths can vary and typically fall into one of three categories: neutral, strong, and weak. Although the neutral grip is the preferred grip, a golfer with weaker or smaller hands may prefer a stronger grip. In a stronger grip, the hands are turned slightly toward the trail side to help bring the clubface back to the proper position when the ball is struck. However, for some players a strong grip may cause the ball to spin too much to the left (for a right-handed golfer), which is referred to as a hook. If you are hooking the ball, review your grip to be sure it is not in a strong position. The club will generally be positioned more in the palm of your hand than in your fingers.

Stronger players may prefer a weaker grip. In a weak grip the hands are slightly toward the target side, which keeps the club from squaring up or closing too soon in the swing. A player with strong hands and tremendous clubhead speed may fare better with this type of grip. However, this grip sometimes causes the ball to spin too much to the right for a right-handed golfer, which is referred to as a slice. If you are having trouble with the ball moving or curving too much to the right, you may want to move your hands to a stronger position.

Differences in Posture and Alignment   Postures will look different simply because golfers have different body types. The most important element to remember is to position the body to allow for the best balance and turning motion. Golfers who have difficulty with balance may prefer a wider stance. Golfers with robust bodies may find that their arms hang slightly farther away from the body than normal. Golfers who wear bifocals may have to position their heads slightly lower to see the golf ball properly. A tall, thin, lanky body may appear closer and more upright to the ball as opposed to a shorter, wider body, which may require more tilt to reach the ball. Most important, the body needs to be in a ready position to move and stay balanced.

Alignment may vary according to the conditions of the course. A ball that lies on a slope will fly in the direction of the slope. The golfer must account for the slope when making the shot. For example, a right-handed golfer playing a shot from an uphill lie needs to know that the ball will have the tendency to fly higher than normal and more to the left. If the ball is on a downhill lie for the right-handed golfer, it will have the tendency to fly lower than normal and sometimes to the right. A ball that lies above the feet on a sidehill lie will have the tendency to fly to the right. Alignment must be adjusted to account for the ball flying right. The player will then line up to the left of the target. How much to the left depends on the severity of the slope. A ball that lies below the player's feet will have the tendency to fly to the right (again, for the right-handed player). The player must adjust his or her alignment by lining up more to the left of the target to allow for the ball to fly right.

Wind can also affect the flight of the ball. If the wind is moving left to right, the right-handed golfer may want to line up farther left of the target to account for the wind moving the ball back to the right. Conversely, if the wind is moving right to left, then the alignment may be to aim slightly right of the target.

Preshot Routine

In any sport the athlete's preparation before starting the activity is the key to success and allows for more consistency. A common complaint from golfers is that they are inconsistent in their game. For most of these golfers the solution lies not in changing their swing but in adjusting their preshot routine. Have they set themselves up for success?

All great athletes have a set of motions they use before executing specific techniques. For example, a basketball player goes to the foul line with a set routine before shooting the ball. She may dribble three times, take two deep breaths, bend at the knees, and then shoot. A tennis player may dribble the ball a set number of times and then throw it up to be served. The point is that a routine allows athletes to prepare, focus on the intent, and relax before execution. Once this routine is set, athletes' movements can be automatic, which results in more consistency. Show me a golfer who hits the ball randomly, and I'll guarantee that he or she sets up to the ball randomly before each shot.

A preshot routine for the golf swing starts behind the ball. Imagine that the target line runs from the target back and through the golf ball. By standing behind the golf ball, you place yourself on the target line. This allows for a more accurate view of your intended direction. Place your hands on the club in proper position as you stand behind the ball. Fix your eyes on the target and then look at your ball. Locate a spot 10 to 20 feet away from the ball that falls on the target line. This is the intermediate target. (Intermediate targets are also used in other sports such as bowling. Bowling lanes have small dots very close to the bowler to aid in aligning the ball before rolling it down the lane.) Identifying a spot closer to the ball helps when lining up the clubface to the target.

As you stand behind the ball locating the proper target line, take one or two deep breaths. (High divers sometimes do this right before they step into a dive.) Walk toward the ball. As you walk toward the ball, you will move to the side of the ball keeping your eye on the target and intermediate target. Tilt your body toward the ball and set your club in place. The clubface is lined up directly to the target. Once you have set your target line, you can position your body parallel to the target line. Now that you are set up over the ball, you may want to waggle the club slightly back and forth or tap your feet back and forth to get into rhythm. This is common among top players.

Your preshot routine does not have to look like anyone else's, but you should repeat it before every swing. Make sure that whatever personal moves you decide to put in your routine are positive actions that allow you to focus on the target, relax your muscles before the swing, and align yourself properly. Having a solid and consistent preshot routine will also help when you are faced with more stressful situations on the course such as hitting over a water hazard. The preshot routine combines the three fundamentals of grip, posture, and alignment into one repetitive action to allow for more consistency on the course.

Give it a go

GRIP DRILL

Hold the club in your target hand. Raise your arm slightly lower than shoulder height. Release all but your index finger. The idea is to practice holding the club with only the index finger and the bottom pad of your hand. If the club falls to the ground, you may not have the club firmly in your fingers. Be sure not to let the thumb help hold the club in position.

CHAIR GRIP

While sitting in a chair, go through the proper steps to position your hands on the club. Start with your target hand. When both hands are in place, notice the position of your hands and the relationship of your hand position to the clubface. As you turn your hands to the left, the clubface turns left; as you turn your hands to the right, the clubface turns right. Feel the grip running through your fingers. Keep the pressure of the grip more on the middle fingers as opposed to the index fingers and thumb. Repeat several times until your hands feel like part of the club.

STRENGTHENING THE HANDS

Wring out a towel that is slightly wet by twisting the ends in opposite directions. Shake out the towel and repeat. Strong hands and forearms will reduce the tendency to tighten the grip. Hands should be firm on the club but not tight, the way they are when you hold a pet, a hair dryer, or a steering wheel.

POSTURE DRILL

Standing sideways in front of a mirror, place your hands on your hips and tilt slightly forward. Notice the position of your back and the back of your head. They should remain in the same line. Your tailbone pushes out and up. Your legs bend slightly to keep your weight on the balls of your feet. Allow your arms to fall from your hips directly down from your shoulders. You may feel as if you are about to sit on a stool. Slap your palms together and notice if your arms fall a hand-width away from the body. Repeat the steps to help form the proper posture habit.

ALIGNMENT EXERCISE

Create a practice station to help build solid alignment habits. Choose a target. Set a club on the ground with the grip end toward you and the clubhead turned out so that it falls on the same line as the target. Place another club about two feet away from and parallel to the club on the ground. The second club should be in the same position, with the grip end toward you and the club-head facing out. The clubs lying on the ground like railroad tracks define the path the club will swing through. Place a third club perpendicular to the second club. This will identify the ball position in the stance. As you set up to the railroad tracks (clubs), the third club will run through the center of your feet (figure 7.6). This will help place you in the proper alignment to your target. Start

7.6   **Alignment exercise.**

from behind the parallel clubs and walk in, setting your body in position to hit a shot. You can use a ball if you are comfortable swinging between the clubs. This can be very helpful when practicing alone because it is difficult to see where you are aligned.

ACHIEVE AND PROCEED: FULL SWING FUNDAMENTALS

- Make habits of the preswing fundamentals—grip, posture, and alignment.
- The preswing fundamentals are the basis for a sound and balanced swing motion.
- In a proper grip the club should be placed in the fingers.
- Your hands control the face of the club.
- Proper posture is considered an athletic position with the body tilted slightly forward, the legs slightly flexed, and the weight on the balls of the feet.
- Align the clubface with the target and stand parallel to the target line.
- Consider developing a preshot routine for more consistency.

Full Swing With Irons

The short game shots referred to in the previous chapters are the starting point of the full swing. The putting and chipping strokes use the shoulders and arms together to move the club. This motion is the same motion that starts the full swing. The slight body turn in the pitch swing carries over to the full swing as well.

The full swing causes the ball to travel the maximum distance, which is different depending on the club you are swinging. The full swing requires full rotation of the shoulders in the back swing and full rotation of the hips in the follow-through. The club moves back and up, creating an angle with the shaft of the club and the player. This helps create more clubhead speed, which is necessary to send the golf ball greater distances. The full swing motion can be broken down into the takeaway, back swing, top of the swing, forward swing, and finish. This series of steps should be executed with the proper rhythm and timing. An important aspect of the full swing is that it is one fluid motion moving through the golf ball to the target. Keep in mind that you have been building your golf swing from the short game shots discussed previously in this book. Building the swing from the putting stroke creates strong fundamental habits that are important to a successful swing.

Full Swing With Irons

Setting up properly is essential to making a swing motion with maximum range of motion and balance. Once you have an athletic stance and your club is in the proper position in your hands, you are ready to start the swing. The swing begins like the putting stroke with shoulders, arms, and hands all moving together as one unit. When the club is halfway back, it will be parallel to the ground and in line with the body, and the toe of the club will point to the sky (figure 8.1a). The shoulders are close to 90 degrees in relation to the ground. The club is an extension of the arms. To start the full swing motion, the arms and the shoulders will move together while the club starts to move away from the ball. The idea in the back swing is to conserve energy to be used in the forward swing. This is not any different from many sports. To throw a ball, the arms and shoulders must turn away from the target and store up energy.

The proper procedure for conserving energy in the golf swing is to turn the shoulders away from the target. As the shoulders turn, the arms reach back so the arms and club are parallel to the ground. Like with many pitch shots, there is a slight rotation in the arms as they are moving back. As the shoulders make a full turn, the target shoulder is under the chin and the trail arm begins to fold, allowing the club to move up. To finish conserving energy in the back swing, fold the trail arm while keeping the target arm more extended and stretched. The club will rest on the thumb of the target hand and point back toward the target (figure 8.1b). At the top of the back swing, think of the trail arm as holding a tray or forming an L.

Most important, as you conserve energy in the back swing and complete the motion, your posture remains the same. Your body must turn and stretch. If you are not very flexible and cannot turn your body to this point without changing your posture, turn only as far as you can without compromising your posture. This is critical to making contact with the golf ball consistently. At the top of the swing, the club is pointing back toward the target on a line parallel to the target. The balance point is felt more on the trail leg. The energy is now fully stored. The turn takes place more in the upper body than in the lower body. Picture a large spring such as a toy Slinky. Stand the spring in a vertical position. Hold the bottom of the spring and wind the top. Notice the coil that is created. This represents stored energy.

The forward swing of the club expends the energy, starting with the lower body. This would be similar to letting go of the bottom of the spring as you hold the top. The hips turn toward the target, bringing the weight and balance more toward the target foot as the arms fall down the path to the ball. As the arms move down and through the ball, they will rotate together. This rotation is called the release. The release will happen as long as the arms are free of tension and moving along the intended target line. At impact, the hips have turned toward the target, the arms extend toward the ground, and the shoulders are parallel to the target line (figure 8.1c).

After the ball is struck, the arms and club extend through the target line and out toward the target while the shoulders turn through, causing the front of the body to face the target. When the swing is complete, more of your weight will be on the outside of your target foot, and the club will have moved up and behind you as your arms end in a folded position (figure 8.1d). If your arms have trouble folding in the finish, it is because the rotation did not take place during the swing. Be sure to check your grip and tension in the swing. Your body must remain balanced as you admire the shot you hit!

8.1a   Halfway back.

8.1b   At the top of the back swing.

8.1c   Forward swing.

8.1d   Follow-through.

The golf swing will vary based on the size, strength, and flexibility of the golfer. Energy is stored when the club moves back because the upper body turns around the lower body. The amount that each golfer can turn may vary. The most important factor is to make the turn without changing your posture. The body turns back and through but should not move up or down during the swing. Most golfers who lack flexibility or strength will try to use their body to move the ball by moving the posture up and down or side to side. This will result in inconsistent contact with the ball and less distance because the chance of hitting the center of the clubface is slim. The player is much better off taking a shorter than average swing while maintaining good posture. The swing may be shorter, but the chances of hitting the ball on the center of the clubface increases, which will cause the ball to travel farther and in a more accurate direction. If strength is a factor, then using a stronger grip as discussed in chapter 7 can be an alternative.

Tempo also will vary with each individual swing. Some swings appear to move faster than others because the overall tempo of the swing is faster. Although tempos can vary, the timing of the swings should be consistent. Timing has to do with the amount of time used to conserve the energy in the back swing and the amount of time needed to release the energy in the forward swing. The time it takes to complete the back swing should be two counts to every one it takes to complete the forward swing. In other words, allow twice as much time for the back swing as for the forward swing. Remember that you store energy in the back swing so you can send the ball its maximum distance. Maximum distance is the result of the club moving at top speed through the ball. Think of sending a rubber band across the room. It takes more time to pull the rubber band back than to let it go. Whether the tempo is fast or slow, the timing should be the same. The most important factor is to swing at a tempo that suits you and allows you to move the club at maximum speed.

Full Swing Rules and Etiquette Before executing your full swing, you are permitted to remove loose impediments (leaves, sticks, and stones) from the fairway or rough without penalty. A deliberate swing at the ball that misses is called a *whiff* and should be counted toward your score. When making a full swing with an iron, golfers commonly take out a small amount of grass after striking the ball, which leaves a mark on the course called a *divot*. It is proper etiquette to replace your divot. Take the grass that was removed and place it back to its original position and step down on it lightly.

What's Your Maximum Yardage?

A full swing is intended to send the ball the maximum distance. The maximum distance each player may get from a given club can and will vary. (See chapter 2 on equipment.) A full set of clubs includes 14 different clubs, each with its own purpose. The closer you are to the target, the shorter the club you should use. Shorter clubs have more loft, which makes the ball fly higher over a shorter distance. The maximum distance the ball flies also depends on the player. A new golfer may not notice a difference in the length of their shots when using different clubs because they lack consistency in their swings. When using a 5 iron, a male recreational golfer who has learned the skills of the full swing may be able to send the ball 170 yards, whereas a female recreational golfer may be able to hit the ball only 100 yards with the 5 iron. Because maximum distance with each club varies from player to player, you should take some time to discover yours.

To discover your maximum distance with each club, take a 5 iron and hit 25 golf balls on a practice field. Determine how far you need to step to measure one yard. Walk to the area of the most golf balls, counting off the number of steps. This will give you an indication of how far you can hit the ball with your 5 iron when using a full swing. Each club carries a difference of 10 yards. For example, if you hit the ball 150 yards with the 5 iron, you should be able to hit the ball 140 yards with the 6 iron and 160 yards with the 4 iron. After you have determined how far you can hit the ball with your 5 iron, figure out the 10-yard difference between each club. This is your distance from a flat lie with no extreme weather conditions.

During a game, factor in the course conditions and the lie of your ball when choosing your club. Different terrain and different conditions may change your club selection. For example, let's say that you typically hit the ball 150 yards with the 5 iron. If you are hitting uphill to a green, you may choose the 4 iron because a ball traveling uphill will fly shorter than usual. The same applies if you are hitting into the wind. Wind strength can vary and will usually affect the shot from 10 to 30 yards. If you are hitting downhill toward the target or with the wind, you may choose to use the 6 iron rather than the 5 iron.

During the game, the ball may lie in some difficult situations—uneven terrain, uphill, downhill, sidehill, or among trees or bushes. In these circumstances, it is best to take less than a full swing to ensure contact with the ball. If you use a full swing in these situations, you may fall off balance or cause the ball to fly in the wrong direction (hook or slice).

Ideally, during the game your focus and attention will be on the target and not on the details of how to make a full swing. Having a consistent routine before the shot as discussed in chapter 7 will also help you develop an automatic full swing when on the golf course. Practicing different aspects of the swing off the course will help build the proper swing habits to allow you to focus more on the target and less on the mechanics of hitting.

The following drills will help you practice the full swing and create the proper swing habits. They can be done with and without a club.

8.2 **Toss the ball drill.**

TOSS THE BALL

Hold a small ball of any kind in your trail hand. Stand sideways to the target as if lining up a regular shot. Throw the ball underhand. Notice the turn in your body as you throw the ball underhand. Also notice the balance on the target side and how you are facing the target after you toss the ball (figure 8.2).

TOE-UP TO TOE-UP

This drill will help you practice the release. Turn your shoulders and swing your arms back and to waist height; your club shaft should be parallel to the ground. The toe of the club should point up, and the bottom or leading edge of the clubface should run straight up and down (figure 8.3). Turn your hips to start the forward swing; your arms will follow and finish extended to the target with the club parallel to the ground and the toe of the club pointing upward. This drill can be done with or without a ball.

8.3 Toe-up to toe-up drill.

SHAFT-UP TO SHAFT-UP

This drill works on leverage and release. Begin in address position and bring the shaft of the club straight up in front of you by cocking your wrists toward you. Swing your arms and the club back to 3 o'clock or half swing position. Follow through to the same position on the target side. This drill can be done with or without a ball.

TRAIL ARM

Fold your trail arm at the elbow, making an L with your arm as you turn your shoulders away from the target (figure 8.4). Pretend you are throwing a ball underhand on the downswing and follow through to the target. This drill can be done with or without a ball.

8.4 **Trail arm drill.**

TARGET ARM

Grip the club with your target hand only. Take a very small swing, keeping your target wrist from breaking down and the club shaft parallel with your target arm (figure 8.5). Increase the length of the swing as you are able to control the club. This drill can be done with or without a ball.

8.5 Target arm drill.

BASEBALL DRILL

Assume the correct golf posture as you grip the club. Place your feet close together and tilt forward from the hips. Make the back swing by turning your shoulders. Just as you reach the top of the swing, take a small step with your target foot toward the target. As you take the step, your arms fall to the ground and complete the swing to the finish position. This drill is done without a ball.

TARGET-SIDE COILING

This drill should be done without a club or a ball. Stand in the correct golf posture. Cross your target hand over your trail hand so that the backs of your hands are together (figure 8.6a). Swing back, turning so your shoulders and back are toward the target. Follow through to the finish (figure 8.6b). The elbows fold, the weight is balanced on the target side at the finish, and the body faces the target.

8.6a-b | Target-side coiling drill.

ACHIEVE AND PROCEED: FULL SWING WITH IRONS

- The takeaway begins with the shoulders and arms together.
- In the back swing, energy is conserved by the upper body turning around the lower body.
- The forward swing starts with the lower body.
- Staying in posture is more important than making a full turn.
- The balance in the swing is on the trail foot in the back swing and the target foot in the forward swing.
- Release happens as long as the arms are free of tension and moving on the correct path.
- Tempo can vary from player to player.
- Timing should be consistent with all swings—two counts in the back swing and one count in the forward swing.
- The distance between clubs is usually 10 yards.
- Establish proper swing habits by repeating various drills.

Full Swing With Woods

The full swing with the woods is essentially the same as the full swing with the irons. The energy is stored in the back swing, and the energy is released in the forward swing. The turn starts with the upper body in the back swing and the lower body in the follow-through. Balance is important and should be more on the trail foot in the back swing and more on the target foot in the forward swing. However, the woods are designed for maximum distance. Most woods will send the ball farther than will most irons. There is some overlap, with more lofted woods achieving the same distance as the longer 2 and 3 irons.

Many players swing inconsistently with longer clubs. Because woods are longer, they produce a longer swing, which may be more difficult to control. If you hit straight with your irons but slice with your driver (the 1 wood), this does not mean that your swing changes when you have a driver in your hand. The difference is in the spin that is created once the ball leaves the face of the club. The driver has the least amount of loft and therefore produces less backspin than, for example, the 7 iron. When a shot slices, the ball is spinning left to right (for right-handed players). When a ball is hit with a more lofted club, such as a 7 iron, the ball has more backspin because of the loft of the club. The backward spin counteracts the side spin of the ball so it is more apt to stay on the correct target line.

Full Swing With Woods

The full swing with woods and the full swing with irons differ mainly as a result of the design of the club. The driver, or 1 wood, is designed to give the player maximum distance. Maximum distance is achieved because the club has the maximum length as well as the maximum size clubhead with the least amount of loft. This club design also influences how the ball is positioned in the setup and the plane in which the club will travel. Irons strike a golf ball on the downswing, giving the ball backspin. Backspin is desirable when hitting the ball to a green because it allows the ball to come to a stop. Most shots to the green will be with an iron, although a driver is used at the start of the hole to give the player maximum distance.

When using the driver, the ball is set on a tee to allow the driver to make contact with the ball on the upswing; this gives the ball more overspin so it will roll once it lands on the fairway. Place the ball on a tee with half the ball sitting above the driver when the club is placed behind the ball (figure 9.1a). The ball should be positioned across from your target heel. Placing the ball on a tee and having the ball played off the heel of your target foot allows you to hit the ball on the upswing, which will give the ball maximum roll when it hits the ground.

Because woods are longer than irons, your back swing will feel slower and longer (figure 9.1b). The club stays closer to the ground longer than the irons just because of the length of the club. This is referred to as the *plane* of the swing. The plane is simply the arc of the swing in relation to the ground. To under-

9.1a A tee is used when teeing off with a driver.

stand the plane of the swing needed for each club, set a driver and a pitching wedge with the sole of the clubs (the flat areas on the base of the clubheads) flat on the ground. Lay each club in each of your hands and notice the difference in the angle the shaft of the club makes in relation to the ground. This angle is the lie of the club. The lie of the club determines the plane of the swing.

It is important to respect the design of the woods and not try to swing them up as quickly as you would the irons. Picture holding a rag mop that has just been soaked in water. The bottom of the mop is very heavy. It would be very difficult to raise the mop away from the ground quickly. Swinging the mop would require dragging it back close to the ground until it has enough momentum to move upward.

9.1b   The back swing will feel slower and longer with a wood.

The technique of the full swing is the same for both irons and woods. The difference lies in the setup position. The setup position for the driver is generally across from the target heel. Some players prefer to play the ball even across from the target foot. We refer to this as *farther up in the stance.* If you find that you are frequently slicing the ball, this ball position may be desirable because it gives the club a longer time to get to the ball, giving your hands and arms more time to rotate the clubface to the square position. Do not place the ball back in your stance when using a driver. The design of the club requires that the ball be positioned more forward toward the target heel.

Fairway Woods   Fairway woods are generally numbered 3, 4, 5, 7, and 9. As discussed in chapter 2, the lower the number, the longer the club and the less loft it will have. Loft is the angle to the face of the club, which gives the ball a certain trajectory or maximum height. The 3 wood is used in the fairway and will produce the most distance of the fairway woods. New players sometimes prefer the 5 wood over the 3 wood. The 5 wood is shorter and more lofted, which assists new players in getting the ball in the air. If you have trouble making proper contact with a 3 wood, consider using a 5 wood. When hitting a ball from the fairway, position the ball just inside your target heel. Because the ball is sitting down and not on a tee, the club will come in contact with the ground earlier, thus moving the ball position back slightly. Position the ball across from the target heel for the driver.

Take it to the course

When to Use Woods

When starting a hole, you do not always have to use the driver. Consider a par 3 hole that is only 150 yards long. If you hit 150 yards on average with your 5 iron, that may be your club of choice for such a hole. Now imagine a hole with a narrow fairway or a water hazard 200 yards from the tee. You may not be able to hit the ball straight enough with your driver to avoid the hazard or land in the narrow fairway. A 3 or a 5 wood may be a better choice to use off the tee. The tee shot is not always about hitting the ball as far as possible. Know how far you hit with your driver so you will know when to use it from the tee.

Just as a driver is not always the most appropriate club for the tee, a fairway wood is not usually a good choice to use when faced with difficult lies. A ball that is sitting down in a hole or on very little grass may need to be struck with an iron to elevate the ball. A severe downhill lie may take away the loft of a fairway wood and make it impossible to get the ball airborne with a wood. A more lofted club such as a 5 or 6 iron would be a better choice. Although distance is the first criterion when choosing a club, the lie of the ball should certainly be checked carefully.

Other circumstances, such as the rough, may require a wood. The rough or longer areas of grass that run next to the fairway can vary from course to course. The grass may be very long, causing the ball to sit down in the grass and making it impossible to get the ball out with anything but a high-lofted club. In some cases the ball may be sitting higher up in the grass. A lofted wood such as a 5, 7, or 9 wood would be a good choice if you need the distance. The wood has more size to the head and can move through the longer grass more easily. The longer grass can grab on an iron and twist the head of the club.

Give it a go

SWISH DRILL

The swish drill works pace and rhythm. Hold a long iron or wood upside down in your target hand, gripping just below the head in the *hosel* (figure 9.2a). The hosel is the place where the shaft meets the head of the club. Assume address position and keep your trail hand on your trail hip. Swing back using only your target arm, making a good pivot around your trail leg. Turn your lower body through to complete the swing as your target arm pulls through and folds up at the finish (figure 9.2b). You should hear a loud swish sound as the club moves through the forward motion. Feel, hear, and experience the even pace of the swing.

TRAIL LEG FORWARD, TARGET LEG BACK

This drill helps you feel your upper body turn around your lower body. It improves how you store energy during the back swing. Place your trail leg slightly forward and bring your target foot back, positioning it on the toe (figure 9.3). Turn and swing your upper body around your trail leg. Your trail leg should stay in position, slightly flexed with the weight mostly on your trail leg in the back swing. Come down on your target heel to begin the forward motion. This drill can be done with or without a club. A ball should not be used.

9.2a-b **Swish drill.**

9.3 **Trail leg forward, target leg back drill.**

FULL SWING FINISH

This drill works on balance. Begin in the full swing finish position with your weight on your target side. From the finish position swing the club back to the top of the back swing and then follow through back to the finished position (figure 9.4). Hold the finish for a count of five. Then repeat the motion back and through. Feel the balance throughout the swing.

9.4 **Full swing finish drill.**

DOUBLE OVERLAP DRILL

The purpose of this drill is to help feel the club staying closer to the ground in the back swing. It will allow you to use more of your arms and shoulders to swing the club rather than your hands. Place your target hand on the club in the correct position. Place your trail hand on top of your target hand. Both hands are now overlapping with the thumbs crossed. Place the club down across from your target heel. Place your body in the proper posture position. Start the club back and notice how the club is an extension of your arms and how the club sweeps the ground on the back swing (figure 9.5). At the top of the swing, keep the club still and finish the swing with the forward motion.

9.5 **Double overlap drill.**

ACHIEVE AND PROCEED: FULL SWING WITH WOODS

- The full swing is the same with the woods as with the irons.
- The main difference is in the setup and swing plane.
- A driver, or 1 wood, is used to start the hole and makes contact with the ball on the upswing.
- The ball position for the driver is across from the target heel.
- Fairway woods are played slightly inside the target heel.
- Woods should not be used from difficult lies.

Recovery Shots

A well-known author in the world of sport psychology, Bob Rotella, wrote a book titled *Golf Is Not a Game of Perfect.* Those who have played the game and painstakingly traveled the path to mastery certainly realize the truth of this statement. Famous PGA tour professional Jack Nicklaus was asked after shooting a round of 66 (six strokes under par in a major tour event), "How does it feel? I bet you hit a lot of great shots." He replied, "I hit maybe one or two that I really liked." We can play this game for a lifetime and never play a round in which every shot turns out just as we intended. Although professional tour players, both men and women, are certainly some of the best ball strikers in the world, even they do not hit every shot to the perfect spot. The difference between the best players and those who struggle to make it to the top is their ability to recover from difficult situations.

The ability to make up for a poor shot can mean the difference between par and double bogey on a hole. Recovery shots are those shots that put your ball back in position to play the hole, shots that give you an opportunity to still score when you may have thought you were destined for high numbers. For example, imagine that you just hit your tee shot in the trees. You find the ball among the trees and manage to hit your next shot onto the green. This will not only frustrate your playing competitors, but it will also give you more confidence in your game. Recovery shots are not just for the highly skilled; they can be done by most players if they know what to do and how to execute the shot in a given situation.

Escape the Trees

The punch shot is a shot that stays low to the ground and rolls once it hits the ground. It is a valuable shot to use when your ball comes to rest in a grove of trees. A full swing in the trees is not a good idea for a couple of reasons. First, a full swing would make the ball travel too high in the air where it could possibly catch in tree branches, thus thwarting your efforts to get the ball back to the fairway. Second, you may not be able to take a full swing if your ball is surrounded by trees and low-hanging branches. Your best plan is to find a *window*, a gap in the trees through which you could send the ball back to the fairway. Look for the largest window to allow for any error in the shot.

Once you have chosen a window, make your club selection based on how low you need to keep the ball and how far you want the ball to travel. Sometimes you just need to get the ball out, not necessarily at the perfect target. Usually a 5, 6, or 7 iron is best for this type of situation. Start by bringing your hands down on the grip closer to the shaft of the club. This will shorten the club, which will give you more control. The ball should be positioned back in the stance toward the trail side. Playing the ball back in the stance decreases the loft of the club, giving the ball a lower than usual trajectory. The lower trajectory will help keep the ball flying below the tree branches and back in play. Keep your weight more on your target side throughout the swing. Your swing length should be roughly 9 to 3 o'clock. We sometimes refer to this as a *half swing*.

Another shot you might use in the trees is the *intentional fade*. A fade for a right-handed player will curve in the air to the right, and a fade for a left-handed player will curve to the left. Let's say you find your ball on the right hand side of a hole, and the hole bends to the right around a grove of trees. To play the shot, you want your ball to start out slightly left but curve back to the right toward the green. Set your alignment where you want to have the ball start out. Hold the club out in front of you and turn the face of the club where you want the ball to end up (in this case you will turn it to the right). A clubface turned to the right is considered an *open clubface*. An open clubface will put a left-to-right spin on the ball, allowing the ball to curve to the right when it is in the air.

For the intentional fade, choose a club with less loft such as a 4, 5, or 6 iron. The less lofted club will not impart as much backspin. Remember the discussion in chapter 9 about swinging with the woods. When you hit a shot with a less lofted club, the ball will have less backspin. The challenge is setting up to the ball with your body aimed to the left and your clubface aimed to the right and taking your normal swing. This takes practice. The key is trusting yourself.

The shot called the *figure eight* is useful when you want to hit your ball over a large obstacle such as a tree. The idea is to get the ball up in the air as soon as possible and as high as possible. Visualize the difference between how a helicopter takes off and how a plane takes off. Most golf shots take off similar to a plane; they start out low and rise. The helicopter can move more vertically right from the takeoff. You may find your ball too close to a group of trees with no window through the trees. In this case, your only option would be to get the ball up and over the trees. If the lie of the ball is good, you may consider the figure eight shot. I highly recommend practicing this shot before using it in your next tournament. My teaching partner and men's golf coach, Greg Nye, is a master at the figure eight. It takes some ability to move the club on the correct path and with the right amount of acceleration with this shot.

For the figure eight shot, choose your most lofted wedge. Position the ball just inside your target heel. The path of the club moves similar to the number eight. First, turn the clubface to an open position. The open clubface will help give the ball more height in the air. In the back swing the club will start to the outside of the target line and loop back toward the body and inside the target line. In the forward swing the club will drop to the inside and swing out. The club then comes back toward the body and drops down in the finish. The result is that the ball will pop high into the air and come down on the other side of the trees.

Intentional Draw   The intentional draw for right-handed players is when the ball curves to the left once it is in the air. For a left-handed player, the ball curves to the right. The same rules apply as for the intentional fade. Set your alignment where you wish to have the ball start out. Hold your club out in front of you and turn the face slightly to the left. This is called a *closed clubface.* A more lofted club such as a 7 or 8 iron would be easier to draw. Take your normal swing once you have decided on your setup position.

Chop and Pop   The chop and pop shot is usually used around elevated greens. When you are hitting to an elevated green, the ball can come up short or even roll off the back of the green. The ball can also end up on a severe uphill lie. When using a wedge off a severe uphill lie, the loft of the wedge is increased, making it possible to hit the ball higher than normal and land it short of the target. In addition, maintaining proper balance in the swing from this type of lie can be difficult.

The chop and pop is much like it sounds. Using a pitching wedge or sand wedge, grip down on the club to make the club shorter and easier to handle. Place the ball center to back of center in the stance. Lean your target leg into the hill for balance. Your target leg will be flexed and your trail leg will be considerably more extended. Your shoulders should be parallel to the green, not to the slope. Your back swing will come up quickly, allowing your forward swing to come down more vertically as you "chop" down on the ball and into the hill. The force of the club and the hill will "pop" the ball into the air and onto the green.

Ski Jump   The ski jump shot can be used whenever you need to send a ball up a short distance but cannot start out your shot high because of a tree limb or other obstacle. You need to have a reasonable chance to hit the ball with acceleration to a sloped area. For example, imagine that your ball lies 20 yards to the right of a green. In front of your ball 10 yards away is a tree with a low-hanging limb. The side of the green has a slope leading up to the green. Your strategy is to punch the ball toward the green and use the slope to slow the ball down. The ball will hit into the slope and jump up in the air and onto the green. If you did not use the slope to slow your ball, chances are good that the ball would have rolled across the green.

To execute the ski jump shot, choose a club that will keep the ball low. Place your hands down on the grip for control. Position the ball toward your trail foot. Keep your stance slightly open as though you were going to hit a long chip shot. The length of your swing will depend on how far the ball needs to go and how much acceleration you need to complete the shot.

Choosing a Club Recovery shots, also known as specialty shots, take practice. There are some simple principles to know about the ball position and club design when choosing the type of shot needed and club best suited for the shot. If you want to keep the ball flying lower than normal, play the ball toward your trail foot or back in the stance. If you want to hit the ball higher than normal, play the ball up in the stance or toward your target foot. The club design affects the height of the ball too. The less lofted clubs will keep the ball lower, and the more lofted clubs will make the ball go higher.

When making recovery shots, woods and long irons are usually not the clubs of choice. The longer and less lofted clubs are typically more difficult to control. The lie of the golf ball can also play a factor in the type of club and shot you choose. A ball that is sitting on bare ground or on very little grass should be played more like the punch shot explained earlier in the chapter.

Take it to the course

Recovery shots can be very useful when playing the game. They can mean the difference between winning and losing a tournament. Always have a plan for your shot and know where you want the ball to go. If you are punching out of the trees back to the fairway, be sure to calculate how much distance you have before the ball crosses the fairway and into the rough (or something worse) on the other side. Nothing is more frustrating than hitting your ball out of a trouble spot and right back into another trouble spot!

Recovery is not always about specific shots you can use to hit your ball back into play. You can also recover from difficult situations by knowing the rules of the game and using them to your advantage. When your ball lands on a cart path, sprinkler head, or any man-made object, you are entitled to "free" relief. These man-made objects are considered immovable obstructions. Take your stance as if you are about to hit your golf ball at a point near the obstruction. Place a tee in the ground where your club comes in contact with the ground. Measure one club length from the tee. Drop your ball with your arm extended from shoulder height anywhere in this area. Be sure to take full relief from the obstruction, but do not move the ball any closer to the hole.

You are the judge as to whether you can hit your shot. A ball may be unplayable. It may be stuck under a tree without a chance of moving it. Many times players try to hit these shots only to find they have taken three swings and the ball is still in the same position. Remember, you want to recover as quickly from the situation as possible. You are entitled to take an unplayable lie. It will cost you a penalty of one stroke, but at least you have not frustrated yourself with two or three swings that miss the ball. You have three options when dropping a ball from an unplayable lie: (1) go back to where you hit your last shot, (2) move the ball back any distance along a line to the hole, or (3) measure two club lengths from where the ball lies and drop the ball. Every situation is unique, so choose the best option for your given situation.

Give it a go

It is common to hear players comment, "I hit the ball great on the driving range, but cannot seem to do anything once I'm playing on the course." Golf courses usually look nothing like practice ranges. Most golfers never practice their swing from difficult lies. They practice at the driving range where the lies are usually flat and the targets are straight ahead. Use the following practice drills to learn to lower your scores.

TRAJECTORY DRILL

Practice hitting shots with the ball in different positions in your stance. The purpose of this drill is to notice the changes in trajectory you can make just by changing the ball position alone. Practice this drill with any of your clubs. Play one shot with the ball in the normal position. Then play one shot with the ball back in the stance and play one with the ball up in the stance. Notice the different trajectories with each of the ball positions. The ball played back in the stance should fly lower than the normal ball flight. The ball played up in the stance should fly higher than the normal ball flight.

ON-COURSE PRACTICE

Take time to play on the course when you are not keeping score. Play shots from the various areas discussed in this chapter. Some courses even have practice facilities that provide these types of situations. That is ideal!

ACHIEVE AND PROCEED: RECOVERY SHOTS

- Knowing how to hit recovery shots can lower your scores!
- The punch shot is used to keep the ball flying low.

- Intentional fades or draws help curve the ball in the desired direction.
- The chop and pop uses the hill to send the ball up.
- The ski jump allows a low-running ball to slow down.
- The figure eight is useful in getting the ball high quickly.
- Ball position changes the height the ball will fly.
- Club selection is important in recovery shots.
- Knowing the rules of golf can help you get out of trouble spots.

Course Management

When playing the game of golf, course management is knowing what to do, when to do it, and how to do it. The first step to playing the game is learning the skills discussed in the previous chapters. The second step is taking the skills to the golf course and plugging them in to playing. When you need to focus on your golf swing, you are learning the skills. When you can focus on a target and the conditions that surround the target with no concern for how you should swing, you are playing golf.

Golf is such a challenging game because of the many variables in golf courses as well as the various environmental conditions you may encounter. You must decide which club to use, what type of shot to hit, and what outside factors may influence the direction of the ball. So much of course management can also be considered self-management. You need to have a healthy perspective of what you are capable of—what you can control and what you cannot control. The important thing to remember is that you have a choice in both how you react to your shots and how you handle a given circumstance. There is much truth in the old adage, "You never really know someone until you have played a round of golf with them."

Before stepping onto the golf course, make sure you have rehearsed your preshot routine. You should have a routine for your full swing, your short game, and putting. The preshot routine is what prepares you to execute the shot. It is where you decide on target alignment and visualize the flight of your ball. The routine helps you to relax and stay focused on the shot at hand. A routine on the course for the full swing may include a practice swing. Just remember that one is all you need. Because the full swing does not change, you do not need to waste your energy or time taking several practice swings before the shot.

You should begin your approach for every golf shot by standing behind the golf ball, determining the target line, walking in and placing the club down behind the ball, and then positioning your body parallel to the target line. Once you are in posture, take as little time as possible to start your swing. Some players prefer to waggle their club or tap their feet to help feel the rhythm of their swing. Spending time staring at the golf ball will only cause tension, making it difficult to execute a smooth swing.

Because a short game shot can be of various lengths, a preshot routine for a short game shot requires practice swings. Decide how many short swings you will need to help you decide on the amount of swing necessary. You may feel comfortable with two to four small swings. If you are close enough to the green, you should walk up to the green to take a better look at the surface and the location of the hole. The more information you can take in from the surrounding environment, the better decisions you will make about the type of shot you need to execute. A routine for putting can also include several small practice swings to help you determine the length of the stroke you will want to make. The order that you review your putt should be consistent with your routine.

Starting the Hole

The first shot is played from the tee box area. It is on the tee box that you establish your plan for the hole. The first place most players look is the tee marker, which indicates the length of the hole and the par for the hole. The hole can be three to four different lengths depending on which tee box you choose to start from. Notice the conditions of the environment. Which direction is the wind blowing? Is it cold or hot? Is the grass wet or dry? For example, if the wind is blowing toward you and the air is cool, the hole may play 20 to 30 yards farther. This is important to know so that you can determine what is realistic for you on this particular hole. How far do you hit the ball? This will mentally prepare you for what may be an appropriate par for you, which may differ from what is listed on the tee sign.

The tee box is also where you determine the strength and weakness of the hole. The strength of the hole refers to the areas that will provide challenges, such as water hazards, fairway bunkers, or groups of trees. The weakness of the hole refers to areas with the least amount of trouble or those that are unlikely to create a penalty.

The strength and weakness of the hole will help you determine where on the tee box to tee off. If the strength of the hole is along the right side, position yourself on the right side of the tee box. This will allow you to hit away from the strength and toward the weakness. Focus on a target near the weakness of the hole to align your shot. Paying attention to the design of the hole is very important (figure 11.1).

Getting off to a good start on a hole can make all the difference in the world to your emotional management. It is not uncommon to hit a ball out of play from the tee box. Because this is the longest shot in the game, the chances are higher of the ball veering off course. Take notice of any white stakes lining the hole. White stakes on a golf course mean out of bounds. If a ball is hit out of bounds, the penalty is stroke and distance. This means that you must take a penalty stroke and play another ball from the tee box. You are now lying three off the tee. The same rule applies when you lose a ball. If you suspect that your tee shot could possibly be lost, play a *provisional* ball from the tee. A provisional ball is a ball put in play when the original ball is either out of bounds or lost. This helps speed up play. You would then proceed to the provisional ball, and it becomes the ball in play. You are now hitting your fourth shot.

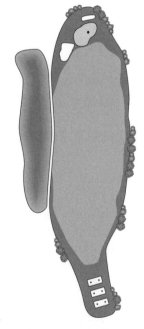

11.1 On this hole, the strength lies to the left and the weakness to the right.

Playing the Hole

You have hit your tee shot. It is now time to start thinking about the next shot. If you mis-hit your tee shot and think about what you did wrong the entire time you are walking to your next shot, you are setting yourself up for failure. You are fueling a negative emotional state. You need to stay focused on your next plan. If you begin to think of your next shot as you are approaching your ball, you will need less time to prepare to hit. The pace at which you play the game has a direct effect on your performance as well as the enjoyment of those who may be playing behind you.

You already have an idea of how far you need to move the ball to your next target. Let's say there is a water hazard in front of the green and you are 200 yards from the green. Be realistic with your game. If you seldom hit a shot 200 yards, play your next shot to land short of the water hazard. You can then play your third shot over the hazard and avoid the stress caused by trying to muscle your shot up to the green, which could land your shot in the water. If you land in the water, you have to drop from the hazard and receive a penalty stroke. You are now hitting your fourth shot over the hazard when you could have been hitting your third had you played smart.

Playing to the Green

You are now approaching the green. This is the part of the game in which many strokes are wasted. If the ball lies near the green, the first question to ask is, Can I putt it? The putt is the simplest form of the golf swing. You can putt the ball as long as the area you need to roll the ball over has little chance of throwing the ball off the target line. If you decide not to putt, the second question is, Can I chip it? You can (and should) chip whenever you have more green to the hole than distance from your ball to the start of the green. If you cannot chip, your last option is to pitch. The surface over which the ball has to travel and the ratio of grass before the green and the amount of green to the hole determine which shot is best.

It is important to review your shot and the conditions surrounding the shot. For example, you may find your ball behind a greenside bunker. As you approach your ball and view your shot, all you can see is a large bunker in front of your ball and a flagstick just on the other side. You can barely see any of the green. This shot can be intimidating from this view. Take time to walk around the bunker and up on the green. Notice the amount of green you have to the hole. In most cases, the amount of green is much greater than it appeared from behind the bunker. The shot now appears much less difficult. As you walk back to your ball, picture the amount of green you have to land your ball. You can now swing with more ease and better focus.

It is wise to walk up on the green when you are chipping or pitching your shot. The slope of the green can determine where to aim, what type of shot to use, and the safest place to hit your ball. In other words, you do not want to chip your ball past a hole when the green slopes toward you. This would leave you with a downhill putt. Controlling the speed of a downhill putt is difficult. You might miss the hole and be faced with a longer putt than your first. An uphill putt is much easier to control than a downhill putt. There is a phrase in golf management: Keep the golf course in front of you. A shot played short of the green is generally easier to hit than a shot that rolls over the green. A putt played short of the hole is generally easier than one that is past the hole. Of course, golf courses do vary, and not all greens have considerable slope.

On the Green

As you walk up to the green, take notice of the direction in which the green is sloping. This is usually easier to see when you are farther from the green as opposed to standing on the green. The slope of the green directly affects the direction in which the ball will roll. As discussed in chapter 3 on putting, this determines the target line. Once you are on the green, walk to the hole first and then back to your ball. Look at the condition of the green around the hole. Which way is the green sloping? What side of the hole is best to have a second putt from in the event that the first putt does not go in? Is the surface hard or wet under your feet? This could affect the speed of the ball when it approaches the hole. In the rules of golf it is not permissible to test the surface of the green by touching it with your hand. You may only touch the green to remove small pebbles, leaves, sticks, and other loose impediments.

Etiquette while on the green is also important to know. You should never walk across a playing competitor's line to the hole. Be aware of where each ball is on the green so as not to step in someone's path to the hole. The grass compressed by a footprint on a green can take as long as 20 minutes to rebound. This could affect the roll of the ball on the way to the hole.

Sloped Shots

Sometimes a ball will come to rest on an uneven playing surface or a slope. Golfers commonly have to hit shots from uphill, downhill, or sidehill positions. Keep in mind that the most important thing is to make a swing that will allow you to stay in balance. A swing without balance can make hitting the ball difficult. Balance can be achieved by taking a half or three-quarter swing. Knowing the rules that apply to various slopes is also crucial to proper ball striking:

1. The ball will fly in the direction of the slope.
2. Play the ball position toward the higher side of your body when set on the hill. In other words, the ball position moves to the top of the hill.
3. Take a wider stance and less than a full swing to maintain balance.
4. Position your body with the slope.

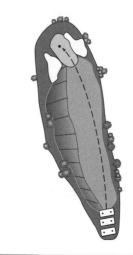

| 11.2 | Slope runs right to left; ball tends to fly left. |

A ball that is on a slope that runs toward the left will tend to fly left (figure 11.2). The amount the ball will fly to the left depends on the severity of the slope. You must therefore aim slightly to the right of the target to compensate for the ball's tendency to travel left with the slope. A ball on a slope that tilts toward the right will tend to fly to the right (figure 11.3). You must therefore aim slightly left to compensate for the ball's tendency to fly right. In both cases, you should play the ball from the center of your stance.

| 11.3 | Slope runs left to right; ball tends to fly right. |

A ball on an uphill lie will tend to fly higher than normal (figure 11.4). Because of the slope, the club's loft will increase, causing the ball to fly higher than normal with a given club. You may want to go down one club to compensate for the extra loft from the uphill slope. For example, imagine that the ball is on an uphill slope and you have 100 yards to the green. On a flat you might use your 8 iron, but because of the uphill lie you may want to change to the 7 iron. The slope will increase the loft of the 7 iron to that of an 8 iron. If the lie is severely uphill, the ball will have a tendency to fly slightly left.

A ball on a downhill slope tends to fly lower and farther than normal (figure 11.5). To compensate, you may want to go up one club. Imagine again that you are 100 yards from the green, only now the ball is on a downhill slope. You may need an 8 iron for the distance, but the 9 iron would be the better choice because the slope will decrease the loft of the club, making the 9 iron like an 8 iron. For either an

11.4　　An uphill lie will cause the ball to fly higher than usual.

11.5	A downhill lie will cause the ball to fly lower and farther than usual.

uphill lie or a downhill lie, the ball position should be to the higher side of your body—toward the target foot for an uphill lie and toward the trail foot for a downhill lie. If the downhill lie is severe, the ball will have a tendency to start out to the right of the target.

When hitting the ball from any kind of sloped lie, use a three-quarter swing to stay balanced. Sloped shots hit incorrectly are usually the result of poor balance and incorrect ball position.

Environment

Weather can affect a golf shot. The wind, rain, heat, and cold all affect the flight of a golf ball. When you are hitting a shot into the wind, keep the ball flying low. A ball hit high in the wind will have a difficult time staying on course and reaching the target. A ball flying low has more control in the wind. For example, imagine that you are 75 yards from the green. You would usually use your wedge to hit your shot on the green. The wedge will make the ball fly high in the air. The best choice would be to use a less lofted club such as a 9 or 8 iron. To play a shot that will fly lower than normal, begin with the ball back in the stance toward the trail foot. You may only need a half swing to get the ball to the target. If the wind is behind you, depending on how strong it is, it may carry the ball farther than normal. You may want to go down a club; if you would normally use an 8 iron, perhaps you would change to a 9 iron and allow the wind to carry your ball to the target.

In rainy conditions the ball will have less roll when it hits the ground because of the softness of the ground. In dry conditions the ball will roll more when it hits the ground. Club selection varies depending on where and what you are hitting to. If you were hitting a shot to a wet green, you would want to use a club that would send the ball all the way to the flag. When the ball lands on a wet green, it tends to stop more quickly. In some cases you may choose to go up one club to allow for the wet condition. In hot, dry weather the ground can become hard, making the ball roll more than usual. In dry conditions you would want to hit your shot short of the green and allow the ball to roll up to the flag. Balls often roll off the back of the green during hot, dry conditions.

Types of Lies

When hitting out of longer grass, play the ball in the middle or back of your stance. The ball will have more roll once it hits the ground. The long grass gets between the face of the club and the ball, which takes away most of the backspin that is usually put on a ball when it compresses against the face of the club. To elevate the ball out of the deeper grass, choose a club with loft, such as a 7, 8, or 9 iron or a lofted wood such as a 7 or 9 wood if you need more distance. When hitting from longer grass that is around the green, be sure to allow for the tendency of the ball to roll when it hits the green. Target a spot farther from the hole to allow the ball to roll to the hole.

A surface that provides very little, if any, grass under the ball is referred to as *hardpan* or a *tight lie.* When hitting from such a surface, remember the phrase *bad back.* These types of lies are considered *bad* and therefore should be played *back* in the stance toward the trail foot. This allows the club to make a steeper descent on the ball and catch the ball first before hitting the ground. A shorter club such as a 6, 7, or 8 iron is best suited for this type of shot.

Elevation

As you play the game, you will gain more knowledge about how the golf ball reacts in different conditions. We have already discussed how to hit off different slopes and different lengths of grass. Elevation is another variable to take into consideration when choosing your club or your shot. When approaching a green that is elevated considerably more than the fairway you are on, the ball will fly at a lower than normal trajectory (figure 11.6). Because it is coming into the green low, it will have a tendency to roll more. Be sure to play the shot short of the intended target to allow the ball to roll up to the target. If you try to hit the ball so that it lands next to the flag, it may roll past the flag and possibly over the green.

When you hit a shot from an elevated fairway to a lower green, the ball will come from a higher than normal trajectory, which will cause the ball to "crash" on the green with very little roll (figure 11.7). You should choose a club that will let you hit the ball farther so that it flies all the way to the target, or you should take a longer swing to ensure that the ball lands closer to the hole.

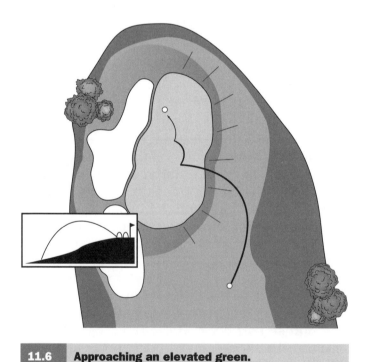

11.6 **Approaching an elevated green.**

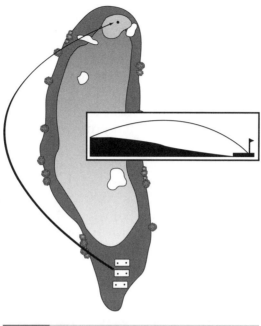

11.7 When hitting from an elevated fairway to a lower green, the ball will come from a higher trajectory.

Conquering Doglegs

Once you learn the skills of the full swing, you are ready to learn how to intentionally make the golf ball fly with a slight curve to the right or left. This is known as hitting a *fade* or *draw*. A situation in which it might be necessary to hit a fade or draw is when the ball lies close to one side of the fairway and the hole bends to the right or left. This is called a *dogleg*. You may want to have the ball fly straight for a certain distance and then curve with the shape of the hole (figure 11.8). This requires some practice and knowledge about what makes the ball curve.

The clubface position makes the golf ball spin or curve once it is airborne. The path of the club makes the ball take off in a particular direction. If the path of

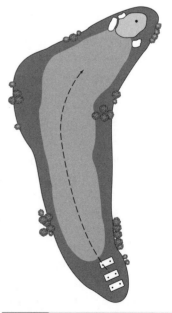

11.8 Use a fade on a dogleg to the right.

119

the club is moving down the intended target line and the clubface is square, the ball will tend to fly straight. If the clubface is open so the heel of the clubface is in front of the toe, the ball will curve right for a right-handed player. If the clubface is closed so the toe of the clubface is in front of the heel, the ball will spin left for a right-handed player.

Intentionally hitting the ball with a slight curve is called *dialing a shot.* To hit a shot with a right to left curve, dial the clubface so that the toe is slightly in front of the heel; then position your hands on the club. Align your body in the direction in which you would like the ball to start. This assures the path of the club, which influences the initial direction of the ball. Now, take a regular full swing. To hit a shot with a left to right curve, dial the clubface so that the heel is in front of the toe; then position your hands on the club. Align your body in the direction in which you would like the ball to start. Now, take a regular full swing.

Making Decisions on the Course

Each shot requires a thought process before club selection and execution. When approaching the ball, note the lie of the ball. Is it on a slope? Is it in short grass or long grass? Consider where you want the ball to go. Is the target uphill or downhill? Also, observe the weather. In what direction is the wind blowing? You may have seen players toss a small amount of grass into the air before hitting their shot. This is how they determine the direction of the wind. Is the target you are hitting to wet or dry? Finally, run through your preshot routine. Select your club, stand behind the ball to determine the target line, and take a practice swing if you wish. Walk toward the ball and place the clubface behind the ball. Lean forward with your upper body. Place your feet last; then start the back swing. Follow the same steps with every shot to make your game more consistent.

Once you begin to play consistently, take notes on each hole you play. Record whether you hit the fairway from the tee. Record how many shots it took you to reach the green. Record if you had the opportunity to chip or pitch on the green and how many putts it took to get the ball in the hole. By doing this, you will begin to see patterns of where your game needs improvement. For example, you may notice on a 9-hole round that you took a total of 30 putts. You want to shoot for a maximum of two putts per green. If you bring your average putts down from 30 to 20, you will improve your overall score by 10 strokes just in putting improvement alone!

Having good course management mostly means knowing what you can realistically do, choosing the appropriate club based on that knowledge, and then trusting your decision once you have made it! You have the choice to be in control of your game. The greatest thing about the game of golf is that your success or failure does not depend on what someone else does. Regard the golf course as your competitor when deciding what constitutes success according to your level of play. Enjoy the play!

ACHIEVE AND PROCEED: COURSE MANAGEMENT

- Know how to find the strength and weakness of the hole.
- Know how the slope of the ground affects the flight of the ball.
- Know how the ball reacts to different lies.
- Determine the maximum distance you get from each club.
- Develop a consistent preshot routine.
- Keep statistics of your game.

12

CHAPTER

Scoring and Tournaments

The game of golf has many variations to the scoring process as well as tournament formats to make the game enjoyable for all levels of play.

Scoring

Golf can be played using many different ways of scoring and competing. The most common is stroke play. In stroke play, each player scores his or her own ball and tallies the results with a total number of strokes for the number of holes played. Most professional tournaments are played with a stroke play format. The total number of strokes for the game is considered the player's *gross score*. Gross scoring is used most often in tournaments with players who have equal playing ability. The PGA and LPGA professional golf tours use the gross score. Top amateur events also use a gross scoring method when playing stroke play events.

For more recreational golf events a handicap system is used. Anyone who plays the game can establish a handicap. The USGA handicap system is a method to equalize competition. A player's handicap is an indication of his or her ability on a particular golf course. The USGA also establishes a course rating and slope rating. These ratings are calculated based on the difficulty of a particular golf course. A player establishes a handicap through a golf club. Most courses have a handicap chairperson and committee to ensure fairness through peer review. Today most scores are recorded into a computer system that calculates the scores. Fifty percent of the total rounds you have recorded are used, and the lowest scores are taken. You need a minimum of five completed rounds to establish a handicap. A total of the handicap differential is added and averaged. The average is multiplied by 0.96. Take off any digits after the tenths, and you have your handicap.

The handicap is a rough estimate of the average score over the par. If a player has a score of 100 and his handicap is 30, his net score is the gross score minus his handicap. Therefore, his net score would be 70. For example, in tournament play player A, who has a 10 handicap, shoots a gross score of 90, resulting in a net score of 80. Player B, who has a 30 handicap, shoots a gross score of 100, resulting in a net score of 70. Player A beats player B in gross score, but loses to player B in net score.

Match play is another form of scoring and competing. This format is used most often to establish club or state champions. In match play the player competes against only one other player in the field on a hole-by-hole basis. Matches are established in the field based on a qualifying round of stroke play. The low stroke finishers are ranked the highest. The highest ranked players play against the lowest ranked players first. This makes it more likely that the two best players will be left after all the matches have been played.

The player who wins the match will play the winner of another match in the field. The tournament is completed when two players are left and play off for the championship. This format usually requires three to four days to complete depending on the number in the field. In match play, each player keeps track of his or her score for the hole. If player A scores a 4 and player B scores a 6, player A has won the hole. Player A is considered one up for the match regardless of the difference in the number of strokes they each had for the hole. On the second hole player A scores a 7 and player B scores a 4. Player B has won the hole. The match is now considered even. On the third hole player A scores a 4 and player B scores a 3. Player B has won the hole. Player A is now 1 down for the match, and player B is 1 up. This continues until one player is up more than the number of holes left to play. For example, if a player is up 3 holes with only 2 holes left to play, the match is over. If the match is tied after the last hole has been played, the match will go on in a sudden death playoff. A sudden death playoff starts on a hole designated by the tournament committee and is played only until a hole is won by either player.

Match play can be fun for recreational play too. Handicaps can be used when playing match play as well. This is very helpful when two competitors are of very different skill levels. For example, if player A has a 10 handicap and player B has a 20 handicap, the difference between their handicaps is 10. Therefore, player B receives 10 strokes from player A. Strokes are given on the first 10 most difficult holes. This is indicated on the scorecard under the handicap line. Each hole is tested and assigned a difficulty level based on the entire 18 holes. The number 1 handicap hole on that particular course is considered the most difficult to play. The number 10 handicap hole is considered the 10th most difficult to play. One stroke is given for the first 10 hardest holes on that particular course. If the number is greater than 18, then two strokes are added to the appropriate holes. If, for example, the players are on the 10th most difficult hole and player A scores a 4 and player B scores a 5, player B receives a stroke from player A and her net score is 4. They tied the hole using the handicap match play format.

Tournament Play

Players have many different choices of tournaments in which to participate to add variety to playing the game of golf. Some of these options include professional tournaments, gross versus net score tournaments, match play championships, scrambles, and best ball tournaments. Most professional tournaments use the stroke play format. Each player is responsible for counting up the number of strokes on each of the 18 holes. A total score is recorded. The player with the lowest score of the field is the tournament champion. If two players are tied at the end of the tournament, they will play off starting on the hole designated by the tournament committee. Play continues until one player has a lower score on the hole.

Gross and net score tournaments award both a low gross champion and a low net champion. The low gross champion in the field is the player who has the lowest score without using a handicap. The low net champion in the field is the player who has the lowest score after taking a handicap minus the gross score. In a match play championship, players are sorted into brackets based on one day of stroke play. The lowest scores are ranked to the highest scores and placed in a bracket. Matches are played until two players remain and play for the individual championship.

Scramble formats most often are used with large golf outings, such as corporate golf outings or fund-raising tournaments to benefit non-profit organizations. A scramble format is best when the participants have different skill levels. A corporate outing generally brings together players of different experience and skill. In a typical scramble, each foursome plays as a team. If possible, teams are organized to even out the competition. A team would consist of a highly skilled player, two moderate players, and a novice player. Each member of the team hits a tee shot. The best shot is selected, and the rest of the balls are picked up and moved to the selected ball's position. Players hit their second shots from the selected position. Again the best shot is selected, and players move their balls to the chosen spot. The hole continues in this format. On the green, players putt from the same position until their balls are in the hole. Only one score for the group is recorded. This usually results in lower scores from the entire field, as well as enjoyment for players of all skill levels.

Several variations to the scramble format can be used, depending on the tournament committee and the variations of skill levels within the field. Variations of the scramble format may include using a certain number of shots from each player on the team. This ensures that everyone is part of the team score. It also creates fairness throughout the field.

A best ball tournament is another form of recreational golf tournament. It can be played as either a gross event or a handicap event. Best ball teams can consist of two, three, or four players, although they are generally two- or four-player teams. The team members play together. Each player on the team scores his or her own ball. The lowest score from the team is recorded after each hole. For example, player A and player B are best ball partners. Player A has a 4 on the first hole and a 6 on the second hole. Player B has a 5 on the first hole and a 3 on the second hole. Their best ball score is a 4 for the first hole and a 3 for the second hole. The round continues until a total best ball score is recorded. The team with the lowest score is the winning team.

A variation of the best ball format uses the handicap system. Players are given a percentage of their handicaps. For example, player A is given an 18 handicap and player B is given a 9 handicap. Player A gets one stroke for each hole. If player A has a 4 on the first hole, his net score is 3 and can be used in the best ball score. Again, the handicap system is best suited for tournament fields of various abilities.

Scoring for New Golfers

When playing on a course for the first time, it isn't necessary to keep score. New players should set their own par. The par assigned to the hole by the course indicates the score most professionals shoot for—it is considered perfect. It is not designed for the novice player. New players who want to experience playing the game on the course should take the par and double it. If you can achieve double par or better, you are doing very well. Take the par given to the hole to determine how many shots you will take to position your ball within 50 yards of the green. For example, on a par 4 hole, take four shots to get 50 yards or closer. If you are not within 50 yards, pick up the ball and move it within 50 yards of the green. Take four more shots or fewer to get the ball in the hole. If you are not yet in the hole, pick up the ball and proceed to the next hole. This will help you keep up with the pace of play on the course and give you experience playing the game. Too many recreational golfers give up the game because they do not feel they are skilled enough to go out on the course. It takes time to develop skills. Use this method for practice and before long you will be hitting every shot and finishing out the hole.

On-Course Games

The typical scoring method for golf is to count every stroke for each hole and add up the strokes at the end of the round. However, there are many variations to playing and enjoying the game. Here are some suggestions.

Match Play With Friends

Two players are required. Each player counts his or her strokes on a particular hole, and the two players compare their scores at the end of each hole. The lower score wins the hole, regardless of the difference in strokes. The player who wins the hole would be 1 up. If the two players tie the second hole and the same player wins the third hole, that player is now 2 up. The player who lost the two holes is considered 2 down. The match continues with the player who is up at the end of the round the winner. When a player is 3 up with two holes left to play, the match is considered over. The losing player may consider putting on a *press*. This is a separate match that would only include the holes played after the press was accepted. A press is a fun way to keep the competition alive when the first match is over. If a player loses the match but wins the press, the players are tied. The players can decide whether they want to play gross score on each hole or use the handicap system.

Scramble With Friends

Play this format when you are playing in a foursome. If takes the pressure off each individual player. Split the foursome into two teams, with more skilled players pairing up with less skilled players. Each player on the team hits a tee shot, and the partners choose the best one. A second shot is hit from the spot where the best shot landed, and again the best shot is selected. Play continues until the hole is completed. The scramble scores of the two teams are compared to decide which team is the winner.

Best Ball

The best ball format can be used with two or more players. If you happen to be playing in a threesome and one player is more skilled than the other two, it can be fun to play the best ball of the two players against the score of the more skilled player. Each player scores with his or her own ball. The lowest score at the completion of the hole is recorded. In some cases, you may want to play two against two. Two people from the same group play against two others. Whoever has the low ball out of the partners wins the hole.

Another option is to play so the low ball out of the best ball receives a point and the lowest high ball out of the best ball receives a point. This way everyone is in the game at all times. You can add a further component by giving a point for the low total of the partners. It is then possible to win up to three points on one hole. For example, team A has both a 3 and a 6 on the hole for a total of 9, and team B has a 4 and 5 on the hole for a total of 9. Team A gets a point for the low score, and team B gets a point for the lowest high score. Because the total of the two teams is tied, no points are awarded for the lowest total. You had better use a scorecard because this can be hard to keep track of!

Nassau

Nassau is a betting game. To begin, the players choose a dollar amount to play for. You need at least two players. For example, if you are playing a $5 Nassau, the winner of the first 9 holes receives $5.

The winner of the second 9 holes receives $5. The overall winner wins $5. Thus, the most you could possibly win is $15. Either match play or standard stroke scoring can be used. This can test your nerves depending on how much money you decide to wager.

Six-Six-Six

The point of six-six-six is to have different partners throughout the round. This works well with players of similar skill levels. You need a foursome to play this format. Partners are determined by matching the player who hits the longest drive with the player who hits the shortest drive. Each 6 holes in a round of 18 is a separate game. Typically, a best ball format is used with the partners. Stroke or match play can be used. For the second 6 holes, partners are determined in the same way except that no two partners can be the same. By the last 6 holes, your partner is the person you have not been paired with yet. Three different matches are played in a single round.

Pinehurst

Pinehurst can be played within your foursome or against an entire tournament field. It is a partner game. You and your partner hit your tee shots. If you hit the better drive, your partner hits the next shot. You then continue alternating until you finish the hole. You will have one score for the two of you. The player with the lowest score at the end of the round is the winner. This can be fun because you can tease your playing partner for putting you in a bad spot or vice versa.

Skins

Skins can be played with two or more in your group or among an entire competitive field. A skin is scored by the player with the lowest score on any given hole. If two or more players have the lowest score for the hole, the hole is considered a tie and no skin is won. Bets can be placed at the beginning of the round. One dollar or any value that is predetermined is thrown into the pool by each participant. There could be as much as $50 in the pool! If there are only two skins for the day, the two people with the skins split the pool, collecting $25 each. This can be a side game to any tournament.

Bingle-Bangle-Bungle

Bingle-bangle-bungle is often played if you have only three players in a group. It can be played with any number, but works well with an odd number because partners are not an issue. Points are awarded for certain shots and added up at the end of each hole. The player with the most points at the end of the round is the winner. Sometimes a value is placed on each point, such as 25 cents. If player A has 12 points, player B has 20 points, and player C has 25 points at the end of the round, then player A owes the difference in points to both player B and player C. Player B owes the difference in points only to player C, and player C wins both from player A and player B. Points are awarded to the first player on the green, the player nearest to the hole once on the green, and the first player into the cup. Because this game does not always favor the lowest score, it is fun game for players of different skill levels to play together.

Side Bets

These are various ways to have fun with your foursome even if your total score has to be handed in at the end of the round. You might be playing against an entire field of players, but have some side bets, such as the following, with just those in your group:

- *Greenies:* The player who is on the green and closest to the hole on a par 3 wins the bet.
- *Sandies:* The bet is won if the player hits the shot out of a greenside bunker onto the green and putts the next shot into the hole.
- *Birdies:* The bet is won when the player scores 1 under par for the hole.
- *Up and down:* The bet is won by chipping or pitching the ball onto the green and putting the next shot into the hole.

Golf is a game to be enjoyed. Always respect the golf course and the rules of the game. How you choose to score, compete, and challenge yourself, however, is up to you. Let it always be what you love.

About the Writer

Denise St. Pierre is director of instruction at the Penn State University golf operation. A former Penn State golfer herself, St. Pierre has also been head coach of the women's golf team for more than eight years. She is a Class A Member of the PGA, a member of the LPGA, and a member of the Board of Directors and chair of the Education Committee for the National Golf Coaches Association.

Sports Fundamentals Series

Learning sports basics has never been more effective—or more fun—than with the new Sports Fundamentals Series. These books enable recreational athletes to engage in the activity quickly. Quick participation, not hours of reading, makes learning more fun and more effective.

Each chapter addresses a specific skill for that particular sport, leading the athlete through a simple, four-step sequence:

- *You Can Do It:* The skill is introduced with sequential instructions and accompanying photographs.

- *More to Choose and Use:* Variations and extensions of the primary skill are covered.

- *Take It to the Court/Field:* Readers learn how to apply the skill in competition.

- *Give It a Go:* These provide several direct experiences for gauging, developing, and honing the skill.

The writers of the Sports Fundamentals Series books are veteran instructors and coaches with extensive knowledge of their sport. They make learning and playing the sport more enjoyable for readers. And because the series covers a wide selection of sports, you can get up to speed quickly on any sport you want to play.

In addition to Golf, the Sports Fundamentals Series will include:

- Soccer
- Basketball
- Bowling
- Softball
- Weight Training
- Archery
- Tennis
- Volleyball
- Racquetball

HUMAN KINETICS
The Premier Publisher for Sports & Fitness
P.O. Box 5076, Champaign, IL 61825-5076
www.HumanKinetics.com

2335